history at

FROM CONFEDERATION TO EMPIRE:
Germany 1848-1914

history at source

FROM CONFEDERATION TO EMPIRE:
Germany 1848–1914

Clive Lodge

Hodder & Stoughton
A MEMBER OF THE HODDER HEADLINE GROUP

British Library Cataloguing in Publication Data
A catalogue record for this title is available from The British Library

ISBN 0340 655 64X

First published 1997
Impression number   10   9   8   7   6   5   4   3   2   1
Year   2002   2001   2000   1999   1998   1997

Copyright © 1997 Clive Lodge

All rights reserved. No part of this publication may be reproduced or transmitted in any form or by any means, electronic or mechanical, including photocopy, recording, or any information storage and retrieval system, without permission in writing from the publisher or under licence from the Copyright Licensing Agency Limited. Further details of such licences (for reprographic reproduction) may be obtained from the Copyright Licensing Agency Limited, of 90 Tottenham Court Road, London W1P 9HE.

Typeset by Wearset, Boldon, Tyne and Wear.
Printed in Great Britain for Hodder & Stoughton Educational, a division of Hodder Headline Plc, 338 Euston Road, London NW1 3BH by Redwood Books, Trowbridge, Wilts.

Contents

Approaching Source-based Questions		1
Introduction		3
1	The 1848 Revolutions	10
2	The German Confederation 1849–62	23
3	The Rise of Bismarck	30
4	Bismarck and Prussian Domination in Germany 1862–71	36
5	Bismarck's Internal Policies 1871–90	49
6	Bismarck's Foreign Policy 1871–90	61
7	William II's Internal Policies 1890–1914	77
8	William II's Foreign Policy: The Early Years	87
9	The Foreign Policy of the German Empire and the Outbreak of War in 1914	100
10	The Germany of Bismarck and William II: A Historical Perspective	114
11	Dealing with Examination Questions	121
	Specimen Answers to Source-based Questions	121
	Preparing Essay Titles	124
	Possible Essay Titles	126
	Specimen Essay Answer	129
Bibliography		132
Index		134

Acknowledgements

The cover illustration is a portrait of Bismarck courtesy of AKG London.

The Publishers would like to thank the following for permission to reproduce the following copyright illustrations:

Hulton Deutsch Collection Limited p16, p17; *Punch* p59.

The Publishers would like to thank the following for permission to reproduce material in this volume:

Addison Wesley Longman Ltd for extracts from *The Revolutions of 1848* by P Jones (1981), *From Bismarck to Hitler* by JCG Roehl (ed.) (1970) and *Bismarck and Germany 1862–1890* by DG Williamson (1986); Allen and Unwin for extracts from *Luxury Fleet: The Imperial German Navy 1888–1918* by HH Herwig (1980), *The Rise of Anglo-German Antagonism 1860–1918* (1982) by P Kennedy and *Germany in the Age of Bismarck* by WM Simon (1968); Berg Publishers for an extract from *The German Empire* by HU Wehler (1985); Cambridge University Press for an extract from *The Unification of Germany* by M Gorman (1989); Edward Arnold for extracts from *Bismarck and Europe* by WN Medlicott and DK Coveney (eds.) (1971) and *A History of Germany 1815–1990* by W Carr (1991); extracts from *Germany 1866–1945* by C Graig (1978) and *The Struggle for Mastery in Europe 1848–1918* by AJP Taylor (1954) by permission of Oxford University Press; extracts from *Prussia, The Perversion of an Idea* by G MacDonagh (1995) reprinted by permission of Reed Consumer Books; Greenwood Press for extracts from *Imperial Germany* by B von Bulow (1914); Hamish Hamilton Ltd for extracts from *Bismarck, the Man and the Statesman* by AJP Taylor (1955); HarperCollins Publishers Limited for extracts from *War and Society in Europe 1870–1970* by B Bond (1984); Macmillan Publishers Ltd for the translated extracts from *Germany and the Approach of War in 1914* by VR Berghahn (1973), *Nineteenth Century Europe* by S Brooks (ed.) (1983) and *The Frankfurt Parliament, 1848–1849* by F Eyck (1968); Penguin for extracts from *A History of Germany since 1789* by G Mann (1974); Princeton University Press for extracts from *Restoration, Revolution, Reaction* by TS Hamerow (1966) and *The Outlawed Party – Social Democracy in Germany 1878–1890* by VL Lidtke (1966); Routledge for extracts from *Imperial Berlin* by G Masur (1970); Rutgers University Press for an extract from *Documents of German History* by LL Synder (ed.) (1958); Simon Schuster International for extracts from *Germany's Self-Destruction* by S Haffner (1989); Unwin and Hyman for extracts from *The Rise and Fall of the Great Powers* by P Kennedy (1988); Wiedenfeld and Nicolson for extracts from *The Rise and Fall of Prussia* by S Haffner (1980), *Bismarck* by A Palmer (1970) and *The Kaiser* by A Palmer (1978).

Every effort has been made to trace and acknowledge ownership of copyright. The publishers will be glad to make suitable arrangements with any copyright holders whom it has not been possible to contact.

Approaching Source-based Questions

The aims of this book are to provide a set of key documents illustrating the formation of the German empire in 1871 and the development of German domestic and foreign policy between 1871 and 1914; in addition, by a series of questions and sample answers, to suggest how the source material can best be analysed and interpreted.

With the adoption by the examination boards of a common core syllabus, questions based on documents and sources now form a compulsory part of their papers. Many boards include such questions in their outline courses and all make source-material questions a dominant feature of their depth studies. In this latter type of paper, it is usual for as much as 50 per cent of the total marks to be allocated to the document section. There is a variation in the type of question set. Some boards require candidates to study prescribed texts, extracts from which appear on the examination paper for analysis. Other boards suggest a wider range of source material for study without indicating specific texts; detailed questions are then set on document extracts which will not necessarily have been seen previously, but which candidates should be able to analyse by reference to their knowledge of the course.

It is important that candidates appreciate the weighting that the examination boards now give to the documentary approach in the study of History. There is a broad measure of agreement between the boards with regard to the integral place that document study now has in the common core syllabuses.

This work gives a range of different types of source-based questions. Some examination questions are essentially a comprehension exercise, testing the candidate's ability to read and understand a historical document. Other questions examine candidates' background knowledge of wider themes or probe their understanding of special topics. The most demanding questions are those which ask for an assessment of the historical value of a given document or for a comparative evaluation of separate sources.

All examination papers indicate the number of marks on offer for each question, the practice followed in this book. These are important as a clear guide to the relative importance of the question in the overall examination paper and show what proportion of the candidate's time should be spent on each question. It is not unusual for poorer examinees to write at essay length on parts of questions that carry only one mark! As a rule of thumb, it is worth bearing in mind that for each mark offered there should be a corresponding point of fact or analysis; this is a broad, working guide and should not be followed slavishly. It is not suggested that candidates waste valuable time and effort trying to find an artificial extra point of their own merely to satisfy an apparent numerical requirement.

Care should be taken, as with full essay answers, to deal with the question as

Confederation to Empire

set. An examinee asked to evaluate the significance of a document will gain little simply from paraphrasing it or giving irrelevant details about its background. As well as showing understanding of sources, candidates are expected, at this level, to have an appreciation of historiography; that is, to know something about the problems involved in writing history. Questions are now frequently set which require the candidate's ability to spot bias, attitude and motive in the writer of a given extract. The specimen answers in this book are intended to help in this regard, but certain general pointers are worth mentioning here. When faced with questions about possible bias in a source, candidates should pose themselves such queries as: Is the writer of the extract evidently angry, bitter, confident, detached, involved? Is the document an official report or a personal reminiscence? Does the passage suggest that it is being written for a particular audience or is it a general statement? Is it propaganda or objective reporting? If candidates train themselves to respond in this way to the sources that they meet in their course study, they will develop the type of observational and analytical skills that merit high marks when appropriately used in examinations.

Another consideration, of no small account to examinees, is that a good grounding in document-based work, by broadening their knowledge and sharpening their appreciation of historical material, will prove of inestimable benefit in their handling of full essays. The virtues of this 'knock-on' effect are very apparent to the examiners, as witness this comment from one of their reports: 'It is most unlikely that the highest grades will be awarded to candidates who do not show an awareness of the importance of first sources and an ability to quite relevantly from them.'

INTRODUCTION

By the end of the eighteenth century there was a sense of common culture among the educated minority of Germans, but no sense of political unity. A German nation-state had never existed and the political pattern of separate German states which had lasted since the Peace of Westphalia in 1648 was shattered by Napoleonic conquest. Napoleon abolished the clerical states in Germany and, in 1806, the Holy Roman Empire. For the first time in the nineteenth century the political map of Germany was redrawn when, also in 1806, he created new states, Württemberg, Baden and Hesse, while at the same time enlarging Bavaria, by a series of forced amalgamations.

At the end of the Napoleonic wars the peace settlement achieved at the Congress of Vienna in 1815 created the German Confederation of 39 states dominated by the Austrian Empire and the Kingdom of Prussia. The form of the Confederation owed much to the ideas of Prince Clemens von Metternich, Chancellor of the Austrian Empire. His main consideration was to preserve the Empire. He particularly feared the development of nationalism, which posed a threat to its existence. Consequently, all expressions of German national feelings were deliberately repressed.

Arguably the Confederation (*Bund*), since it almost completely lacked a centralised authority, was no more than a rationalised version of the Holy Roman Empire. It was to have a Federal Diet of 17 members, representing the 39 states, but the members of the Diet were simply delegates acting on instructions from the state governments. The Diet met in Frankfurt under the chairmanship of the Austrian delegate. The position of the smaller states was safeguarded, since to make constitutional changes an assembly representing all the states had to be summoned and decisions had to be unanimous.

The 1815 peace settlement restored power to the princely families, but the way in which they governed their states varied considerably. In Prussia, representative provincial assemblies were created in 1823 but, in fact, all power remained in the hands of the king. In contrast, Baden developed a liberal constitution with a lower house of parliament elected on a property qualification. Debates in this lower house aroused such interest in other German states that many German liberals travelled to Karlsruhe simply to observe them. Liberal activities of this nature were limited, however, since the 1815 settlement gave Metternich, as the dominant statesman of the Confederation, the power to intervene in German affairs. His name became a symbol of resistance to change. Although the historian, A.J.P. Taylor, dismissed Metternich as 'a very silly man', it was the Metternich system which prevailed not only in the German Confederation but throughout central

Confederation to Empire

Europe, thanks to the Holy Alliance of Austria, Russia and Prussia.

Nevertheless there were liberal and nationalist movements in some of the German states after 1815. In 1830 revolution in France overthrew the restored Bourbon monarchy and this inspired outbreaks of violence in states such as Brunswick. However, the incidents were few in number and the effects limited. A minority of radicals had spoken of national self-determination and even of a German democratic republic. In response, repression throughout the German states was fierce, even in traditionally easy-going Bavaria. Hundreds were sentenced to death, although the sentences were usually commuted to imprisonment.

In March 1848, again after revolution in France, a middle-class rising in Vienna led to the overthrow of Metternich. At the same time, governments in the various German states were surrendering to revolutionary pressure. [Chapter 1.] The 1848 revolutions had no single cause; they were the result of political, economic and social factors.

In May 1848, following concessions made by all the state Governments, even the Prussian, elections were held throughout Germany to produce a national parliament to sit in Frankfurt. This parliament represented almost exclusively the liberal middle classes and failed to make the most of its opportunity. The representatives were unable to produce decisions before the princes had recovered their self-confidence. By the time the Frankfurt Parliament developed a constitution for the new Germany, conservative forces had triumphed in Prussia. Fearing the possibility of social revolution, the middle-class liberals were unwilling to challenge the powers of the monarchs. Consequently they failed to establish a liberal, united German state.

Following the failure of the liberals, Prussia made a bid to replace the Austrian Empire as the leading power among the German states through the Erfurt Union in 1850. However, the new Habsburg Emperor, Franz Joseph, with the backing of the Russian Tsar Nicholas I, was able to re-establish the old Federal Diet under Austrian dominance.

There was nearly open war between Prussia and the Austrian Empire when Prussia sent troops into Hesse-Cassel. The Elector of the state appealed to the Diet and indirectly to the Austrians. Prussia gave way under pressure and recognised the pre-1848 status quo by signing the so-called Punctuation of Olmütz.

In Prussia itself, a constitution had been granted by royal patent in 1848. A parliament was elected by a three-class electoral system in which the top five per cent of taxpayers elected one third of the deputies, a situation which lasted in Prussia until 1918. [Chapter 2.] In the 1850s the influence of Prussia in the Confederation steadily increased. This was largely due to economic developments, and in particular to the Customs Union (*Zollverein*) which included most of the German states – except the Austrian Empire – and was administered by the Prussian kingdom. The uneasy relationship between Prussia and the Austrian Empire persisted until Bismarck was appointed Prussian Chancellor in 1862.

Introduction

Otto von Bismarck had been elected to the Prussian United Diet in 1847 and to the Prussian Parliament in 1848, establishing a reputation as an extreme conservative. [Chapter 3.] Between 1851 and 1862 he pursued a diplomatic career. Initially he served the Prussian king as representative to the Federal Diet from 1851 to 1859. He was then ambassador to Russia from 1859 to 1862, followed by a short period as ambassador to Napoleon III's court in France. He was appointed Chancellor in 1862 by King William I when the King faced apparently insurmountable opposition in parliament over planned military reforms.

Bismarck remained in office, almost unchallenged, until he offered his resignation to William II in 1890. The opposition of the Prussian Parliament was overcome by the success of Bismarck's foreign policy. He felt that inside Germany there was no place for both Prussia and the 'worm-eaten old man-of-war', the Austrian Empire. His policy was based on the creation of a Prussian-dominated German Empire and he achieved this in three wars – in 1864 against Denmark, in 1866 against the Austrian Empire and in 1870–1 against France. [Chapter 4.]

Traditionally Bismarck has been credited with achieving German unification. [Chapter 10.] In many respects this is a misrepresentation. He made no attempt to include the Germans of the Habsburg Empire in his creation. In part this was because they were predominantly Catholic and he did not want them to threaten the Protestant majority in the new German Empire. In any case, his intention was to expand Prussian influence, not satisfy the aspirations of German nationalists. After 1871 he waged an unsuccessful battle, the *Kulturkampf* ('struggle between cultures') against the Catholic minority in the German Empire. [Chapter 5.] Bismarck argued that the first loyalty of the citizen should be to the state and he distrusted Catholics because of their obedience to a Pope who, since 1870, had claimed to be infallible. Similarly, because the German Social Democratic Party (*SPD*) was part of an international movement, he introduced anti-socialist legislation which, however, did not succeed in curbing the growth of the *SPD*.

Some writers, like William Shirer, have argued that there is an essential continuity in German history. Bismarck created a German Empire by waging aggressive wars, a policy that was continued by William II and later by Hitler. In contrast, it can be argued that by 1871 Bismarck had achieved the objective of a Prussian-dominated German Empire – ignoring the Germans who formed 33 per cent of the population of the Austrian Empire – and that for the next 19 years he aimed to preserve his creation by a policy of maintaining peace in Europe. [Chapter 6.]

Following the defeat of the Habsburg Empire in 1866, Prussia had deliberately taken no Austrian territory and Bismarck was soon able to re-establish good relations with the Austrian government. In contrast, the peace treaty with France in 1871 had involved a Prussian takeover of Alsace and Lorraine. Afterwards Bismarck feared a French war of revenge to recover these provinces, and thus one of the principles of his foreign policy after 1871 was to keep France isolated and therefore less dangerous. To further this policy he signed an alliance with Austria and Russia, the Three Emperors' League (*Dreikaiserbund*) in 1873. When relations between Russia and Austria were ruptured following the 1878 Russo-Turkish War, Bismarck signed a secret pact with Austria, the Dual Alliance, in 1879. He was able to secure a renewal of the *Dreikaiserbund* in 1881 but, because of continued Austro-Russian rivalry in the Balkans, Alexander III of Russia refused to renew it in 1887. Subsequently, Bismarck signed the Reinsurance Treaty with Russia, ignoring the fact that its terms ran counter to the perceived interests of his ally, Austria.

After the three-month reign of his father, Frederick III, William II became Kaiser of Germany in 1888. Initially his relations with Bismarck were cordial. However, Bismarck, who had served his grandfather, William I, for 25 years soon found the new relationship a strain. Bismarck offered his resignation in 1890 only to be surprised and annoyed when it was accepted.

This point marked a distinct change in the conduct of both internal and foreign policies. Bismarck's conduct of domestic affairs may not always have been successful but he pursued his objectives consistently. William II appointed four Chancellors between 1890 and 1914 – Caprivi, Hohenlohe, von Bülow and Bethmann-Hollweg – and ironically the only consistent feature of their internal policies was inconsistency. [Chapter 7.]

The fall of Bismarck had been provoked by a crisis in the relationship between the *Reichstag* and the Imperial government. Finding a solution to this problem proved beyond the capabilities of his successors. Gordon Craig argues that politics came to resemble a war:

> in which the Chancellor, the *Reichstag*, the Prussian ministries, the state governments, the Imperial court, the organised economic interests and various cabals contended with each other.

In this situation, William II was more a hindrance than a help, periodically embarrassing his government by irresponsible actions. The change in the conduct of foreign policy came with the adoption of the New Course. [Chapter 8.] Initially the Reinsurance Treaty with Russia was not renewed by Chancellor Caprivi in 1890. From that date on, a policy of *Weltpolitik*, the pursuit of world power status, was followed by the German Empire, though not systematically. It was claimed by Chancellors like von Bülow that Germany should have a position in the world which genuinely reflected her military and industrial power. In 1898 the first Naval Laws were passed by the *Reichstag* and from the beginning of the twentieth century the growth of the German navy was increasingly identified as provocative even by pacifically-inclined Liberal and Conservative governments in Britain. [Chapter 9.] There were periods of negotiation between Britain and Germany to try and resolve the problem, but these attempts finally broke down with the failure of the Haldane mission in 1912.

Introduction

In this same period, Germany's attempts to increase her influence in North Africa produced two crises over Morocco in 1905 and 1911. These worsened Franco-German relations, while leading to a closer association between Britain and France. Meanwhile, German relations with the Russian Empire also deteriorated owing to the exclusion of Russian wheat from Germany by high tariffs and ever greater German support for the Ottoman Empire.

Germany's failure to pursue a consistent foreign policy was a consequence of its internal divisions. Grand Admiral Tirpitz and his ship-building allies looked only towards naval conflict with Britain and deplored the hostility to France and Russia, while the professional soldiers and their capitalist allies wanted a continental war especially with France. Von Schlieffen, the Chief of the German General Staff, advocated war with France as early as 1905 – and deplored naval rivalry with Britain. The Social Democrats and the Centre Party were friendly towards Britain and France and identified Russia as the potential enemy.

Historians have debated the causes of the First World War ever since it ended. At different times blame has been attributed to each of the major powers. However, since 1961, Fritz Fischer and other German historians have argued consistently that the German Empire was planning a war of conquest and that this was the principal factor which turned the assassination of Archduke Franz Ferdinand in June 1914 into a major European conflict. [Chapter 9.]

Chronology of the Period 1848–1914

1848	*March*	Uprisings throughout the German Confederation
	March–April	The meeting of the Frankfurt Vorparlament
	May	The opening of the German Constituent National Assembly
		Prussia invaded Denmark in protest at the incorporation of Schleswig Holstein in the Danish kingdom at the request of the National Assembly
	August	Armistice of Malmö between Prussia and Denmark
1848–9	*October–March*	Debate in the National Assembly on the future constitution of a United Germany
	March	The Assembly offered the throne of Germany to Frederick William IV of Prussia
	April	Frederick William IV rejected the crown of Germany, he planned a Union of Princes, the Erfurt Union
1850		The Erfurt Union broke down
		The Treaty of Olmütz re-established the German Confederation under Austrian leadership
		Bismarck became Prussian ambassador to the Confederation
1852–4		Crisis over the Zollverein, Prussia rejected the Austrian attempt to join
1859		Bismarck became Prussian ambassador to Russia
1861		Frederick William IV died, succeeded by William I
1862		Bismarck became Prussian ambassador to France and in a few months Prussian Prime Minister
1863		The Convention of Alvensleben concluded between Russia and Prussia
1864		The German–Danish War, the Peace of Vienna by which Denmark ceded Schleswig, Holstein and Lauenburg to Prussia and Austria
1866		The Austro-Prussian War, ended in Prussian victory
1866–7		The formation of the North-German Confederation under Prussian domination
1870–1		The Franco-Prussian War
		The foundation of the second German Empire with William I of Prussia as German Emperor
		Bismarck became Chancellor of Germany
1873		The signing of the Dreikaiserbund between the German, Austrian and Russian empires
1873–5		The Kulturkampf, the struggle between the German Empire and the Catholic Church

Introduction

1875		The apparent threat of war between Germany and France
1878		The passage of the Anti-Socialist Law
		The Congress of Berlin and the breakdown of the Dreikaiserbund
1879		Bismarck concluded the Dual Alliance between the German and Austrian empires
		Germany introduced protective tariffs
1881		The Dreikaiserbund was renewed
1887		Alexander III of Russia refused to renew the Dreikaiserbund
		Bismarck concluded the Reinsurance Treaty with Russia
1888		Death of William I, succeeded by Frederick III who died within three months
		The succession of William II
1890		Bismarck ceases to be Chancellor, he died in 1898 succeeded as Chancellor by Caprivi
		The repeal of the Anti-Socialist Law
1893		The army increased by 83 000 men
1894		Britain and Germany signed the Heligoland Treaty
		The dismissal of Caprivi, succeeded by Hohenlohe
1896		The Kruger telegram
1898		The passage of the first Navy Law
1900		Hohenlohe was dismissed as Chancellor and succeeded by von Bülow
1904		Anglo–French differences were resolved, the Entente Cordiale
1905		The Björkö Treaty concluded by William II and Nicholas II, rejected by their respective governments
1906		The failure of German policy at the Algeçiras Conference, the end of the first Moroccan crisis
1908		Scandal in Germany over William II's *Daily Telegraph* article
		A crisis in the Balkans over the Austrian take-over of Bosnia Herzegovina supported by Germany
1909		von Bülow dismissed as Chancellor and replaced by von Bethmann-Hollweg
1911		The German warship 'Panther' provoked the second Moroccan crisis
1912–13		The two Balkan Wars
1914	June	Archduke Franz Ferdinand assassinated in Sarajevo
	August	Germany invaded Belgium

1 THE 1848 REVOLUTIONS

The combination of a number of differing factors led to the outbreak of revolutions in the German Confederation in 1848. There was considerable discontent among the German middle classes. Many of them wanted more liberal constitutions in order to be able to influence the state governments; many others wished for the creation of a German nation-state. At the same time there was a growing sense of insecurity among them. The majority of German university graduates looked to the civil service to provide a future career and there were no longer sufficient posts [A]. Among the working classes the artisans (*Handwerkehr*), who felt threatened by increased industrialisation, were to prove the most militant group in 1848 [B]. Also during the period, a large number of peasant families experienced a fall in their living standards because of an increase in peasant numbers (east of the River Elbe this situation was worsened by the activities of efficient landowners, who were reducing peasants to the status of landless labourers [C]), while for the small industrial working class both living and working conditions were invariably harsh [D]. The situation of all these groups deteriorated as a result of a series of poor harvests, beginning with potato blight in 1845 and followed by low wheat production and consequently higher prices in 1846 and 1847 [E].

Within the Confederation, discontent first showed itself in political protests against the influence of Lola Montez, the mistress of King Ludwig of Bavaria. The rulers of most German states also felt threatened following the overthrow of King Louis Phillipe in Paris in February 1848 and the flight of Metternich from Vienna a month later.

There was trouble in many parts of Prussia [F]. On 21 March 1848, after popular demonstrations, King Frederick William IV paraded through the streets of Berlin wrapped in a German flag and soon appointed a new liberal administration in Prussia headed by Camphausen and Hansemann [G]. Throughout the other German states the rulers, in similar moves, introduced more liberal constitutions. As early as 5 March, 51 German liberals met in Heidelberg and resolved to summon a national *Vorparlament* (pre-parliament). This assembly met in Frankfurt with 574 representatives from most of the states in the Confederation and called for the election of a national assembly to draw up a constitution for a German state.

The national assembly was elected and opened its proceedings in Frankfurt in May. The German states had not adopted a common

The 1848 Revolutions

franchise but most had excluded the poor, with the result that the majority of the representatives came from the educated middle classes. Over 80 per cent of representatives were graduates, mostly in law; there was just one peasant and four artisans [H].

Throughout the Confederation governments made concessions. Many rural grievances were removed and public works were started to help deal with the problems of unemployment. Public order, however, was restored by a mixture of concession and coercion. For example, a working-class street demonstration was violently put down by the new middle-class Civic Guard [I].

In Frankfurt the Parliament began to debate the future of Germany. The position of the Parliament looked powerful but in reality it was still dependent on the state governments. The majority of parliamentarians were afraid of the popular demands for social and economic reforms [J–L] and were therefore determined to preserve the monarchy.

The true position of the Frankfurt Parliament was revealed by the Schleswig-Holstein question. The Frankfurt nationalists regarded these states as unquestionably German. Frederick VII of Denmark, who ruled the Duchies, intended to absorb them into his Danish kingdom. The Frankfurt representatives looked to Prussia to defend German interests and the Duchies were occupied by Prussian troops between April and May. This action provoked opposition from Russia and Britain. Consequently, Prussia accepted the Truce of Malmö on 26 August and withdrew her troops. The outcome demonstrated both the international weakness of Prussia and the frailty of the Frankfurt Parliament, which first rejected the Truce and then accepted it three days later. This action certainly undermined the Parliament's prestige.

Meanwhile there were continuing divisions within the Parliament over the future of Germany. When the Parliament first met it seemed that the Habsburg Empire was breaking up and there would be no problem in establishing a Germany embracing all Germans (*Grossdeutschland*) [M]. However, by the end of 1848 Franz Joseph had been installed as a new and vigorous Habsburg Emperor and the revolutionary movements in the Empire were being suppressed. So the Frankfurt assembly voted for a Germany excluding Habsburg territories (*Kleindeutschland*). In fact, by this time throughout the Confederation the state rulers were regaining their confidence. It was not until the spring of 1849 that the Parliament devised a constitution for Germany [N]. It was also decided by a small majority to offer the crown of the new Germany, excluding Habsburg territories, to Frederick William IV of Prussia.

But the situation in Prussia had changed considerably. The army had asserted control in Berlin and the King had dissolved the newly elected Prussian assembly. In December 1848 he had issued his own constitution so that Prussia became a constitutional monarchy not by the will of the

Confederation to Empire

people but by royal decree. Concessions were made both to the artisans and the peasantry [O], winning both groups to the support of the monarchy. So when Frederick William was offered the crown of Germany by the parliamentarians he despised, he rejected the offer [P].

State after state now withdrew its representatives from Frankfurt while at the same time rejecting the proposed German constitution. Defiantly, a rump of radicals removed themselves to Württemberg only to be dispersed by royal troops.

The Frankfurt Parliament had never had more than moral authority. Real power had always remained with the rulers of the German states, particularly as their armies stayed loyal to them. The majority of parliamentarians had never questioned the continued existence of a strong monarchy, which was necessary to protect them from the dangers of social and economic revolution [Q]. Thus the refusal of the rulers of Prussia and the Austrian Empire to accept the proposed changes meant the failure of the national and liberal revolutions. There was no chance of a successful political revolution without a successful social revolution [S–U].

Despite the failure of the revolutions there were positive results. The remnants of feudal oppression had been removed from the peasantry and freedom given to the Jews. At the same time the concept of a Prussian-led German kingdom had been promoted and in a sense the way prepared for Bismarck [R].

A The discontent of the middle classes as seen by the Governor of the Rhine Province in February 1844

The disgruntlement and dissatisfaction which are becoming evident in this province do not emanate from the lower classes, but from the so-called educated groups ... which desire to put their ideas about freedom of the press and popular representation into practice at any cost. To this class belong mostly lawyers, doctors and merchants, who hope by the means which they advocate to achieve a greater importance, for no one believes that they have only the welfare of the country in mind, as they maintain. Yet they all belong more or less to the well-to-do class of society, and they are far from being in sympathy with communistic tendencies.

From T.S. Hamerow: *Restoration, Revolution, Reaction* (1966)

B Artisan reaction to industrialisation in the view of a modern historian

The growth of industrialism presented a serious threat to the social equilibrium of Central Europe, for it undermined the way of life of

The 1848 Revolutions

millions still dependent on a pre-capitalistic organisation of production. The rulers of Germany, impressed with the economic and military advantages offered by the factory system, overlooked the disruptive tendencies which came in its wake. Familiar with guild traditions of conservation and orderliness, they remained blind to the cumulative effects of years of suffering on the lower classes. And so the artisans, having exhausted all peaceful means of influencing the course of government policy, driven to despair by the prospect of economic annihilation, broke at last with established authority and sought salvation in a new political order.

From T.S. Hamerow: *Restoration, Revolution, Reaction* (1966)

C   The revolt of the peasantry
The lack of capital, the inadequacy of reform legislation, the growth of latifundia [large estates], the land-hunger induced by over-population, all in a combination constituted an insuperable obstacle to the creation of an independent peasantry in Germany. They engendered among the rural masses a growing dissatisfaction with freedom which reached its culmination in the great agrarian uprisings of the spring of 1848.

From T.S. Hamerow: *Restoration, Revolution, Reaction* (1966)

D   Prince Felix Lichnowsky tells the Prussian United Diet in 1847 about the plight of the Silesian weavers
The unfortunate weavers ... when they were no longer able to support themselves by their usual occupation, were forced to work with cotton. Not only in Silesia but also in Westphalia, as I learned only yesterday from Westphalian manufacturers, thousands of workers turned from linen to cotton. There arose consequently such an over-production that neither employers nor employees could survive. Numerous factories were forced to shut down, others went into bankruptcy. Among these were very many well-intentioned, kind owners who were reluctant to exploit their workers, although their own deficits mounted. Competition declined, and the freedom of the worker disappeared, for the more abundant and varied the articles being produced, the more independent the position of the worker. Heartless manufacturers oppressed the poor workers, who no longer had the choice of seeking employment with a more humane owner.

From T.S. Hamerow: *Restoration, Revolution, Reaction* (1966)

Confederation to Empire

E The effect of failed harvests on food prices in Hamburg, based on statistics published in 1892

	Wheat	Rye	Barley	Oats
	Price in marks per ton			
1841	100.0	100.0	100.0	100.0
1843	103.1	83.3	98.7	86.4
1846	129.6	91.7	115.6	111.9
1847	151.8	120.8	185.7	149.1
1848	134.0	82.7	124.7	110.2
1849	100.0	53.5	103.9	69.5

From Peter Jones: *The Revolutions of 1848* (1981)

F Trouble in Prussia, a report in the newspaper *Bayerische Landbötin* on 30 March 1848

In most cities of the Rhine Province [Prussia] more or less violent scenes have occurred, as for example in Cologne, Dusseldorf, Krefeld, Bonn, Coblenz and especially in the factory districts of the Berg highlands, where blood has actually flowed in some instances.

From T.S. Hamerow: *Restoration, Revolution, Reaction* (1966)

G Frederick William IV in Berlin in March 1848, as seen by a contemporary observer

In the course of the morning of 21st the King appeared in the streets on horseback with the German colours, black, red and gold, round his arm. He was greeted with tumultuous applause ... he stopped and said 'I am truly proud that it is my capital, where so powerful an opinion has manifested itself. This day is a great day and ought never to be forgotten. The colours I wear are not my own; I do not mean to usurp anything with them ... I want liberty; I will have unity in Germany'. He spoke again of German unity in a proclamation issued on the same day, 'From this day forth the name of Prussia is fused and dissolved in that of Germany'.

From S. Brooks (ed.): *Nineteenth Century Europe* (1983)

H Elections for the Frankfurt Parliament 1848, reported in *Bayerische Landbötin*

The incomprehensible unconcern which many potential voters manifest by absenting themselves at the time of the election is deplorable ... In one precinct of approximately 400 eligibles only 106 voted, in another of about 600 only a little more than 200 participated. What are we to expect from the rural districts, when in the capital there are so many completely ignorant incompetent slackers?

From T.S. Hamerow: *Restoration, Revolution, Reaction* (1966)

The 1848 Revolutions

I Conservative reaction after the middle-class Berlin Civic Guard fired on working-class demonstrators, reported in the conservative newspaper *Neue Prussische Zeitung* in October 1848

The Berlin Civic Guard seems now to have reached the conclusion that there are situations and occasions when it is permissible to fire not only on the people, but even on 'the sovereign people itself'. As long as the brutal soldiery maintained 'law and order' its first duty was to allow itself to be stoned to death peacefully. But as soon as such an attack is directed against the Civic Guard it becomes high treason against the sovereignty of the people and must be suppressed in blood. And yet the attacks and insults to which the soldiers had been exposed were just as great and the soldiers themselves are children 'of the same sovereign people'.

From T.S. Hamerow: *Restoration, Revolution, Reaction* (1966)

J The threat of the German peasant, as seen in 1848 by a doctor from Kalbe who supported the democratic ideal

If there is any cause at all to fear the proletariat, then it is of the agricultural proletariat that we must especially beware ... It has aroused the most frightful passions in the heart of man, and it has bred a barbarism which may carry all the achievements of civilisation to the grave. Let us therefore carry the Middle Ages to the grave.

From T.S. Hamerow: *Restoration, Revolution, Reaction* (1966)

K The Communist Manifesto
1. Abolition of property in land and application of all rents of land to public purposes.
2. A heavy progressive or graduated income tax.
3. Abolition of all right of inheritance.
4. Confiscation of the property of all emigrants and rebels.
5. Centralisation of credit in the hands of the State, by means of a national bank with State capital and an exclusive monopoly.
6. Centralisation of the means of communication and transport in the hands of the State.
7. Extension of factories and instruments of production owned by the State; the bringing into cultivation of waste-lands, and the improvement of the soil generally in accordance with a common plan.
8. Equal liability of all to labour. Establishment of industrial armies, especially for agriculture.
9. Combination of agriculture with manufacturing industries; gradual abolition of the distinction between town and country, by a more equable distribution of the population over the country.

Confederation to Empire

10 Free education for all children in public schools. Abolition of children's factory labour in its present form. Combination of education with industrial production.

From K. Marx and F. Engels: *Manifesto of the Communist Party* (January 1848)

L Events of 1848
(i) The army and the people clash before the Royal Palace, Berlin

The 1848 Revolutions

(ii) The Frankfurt Parliament in session

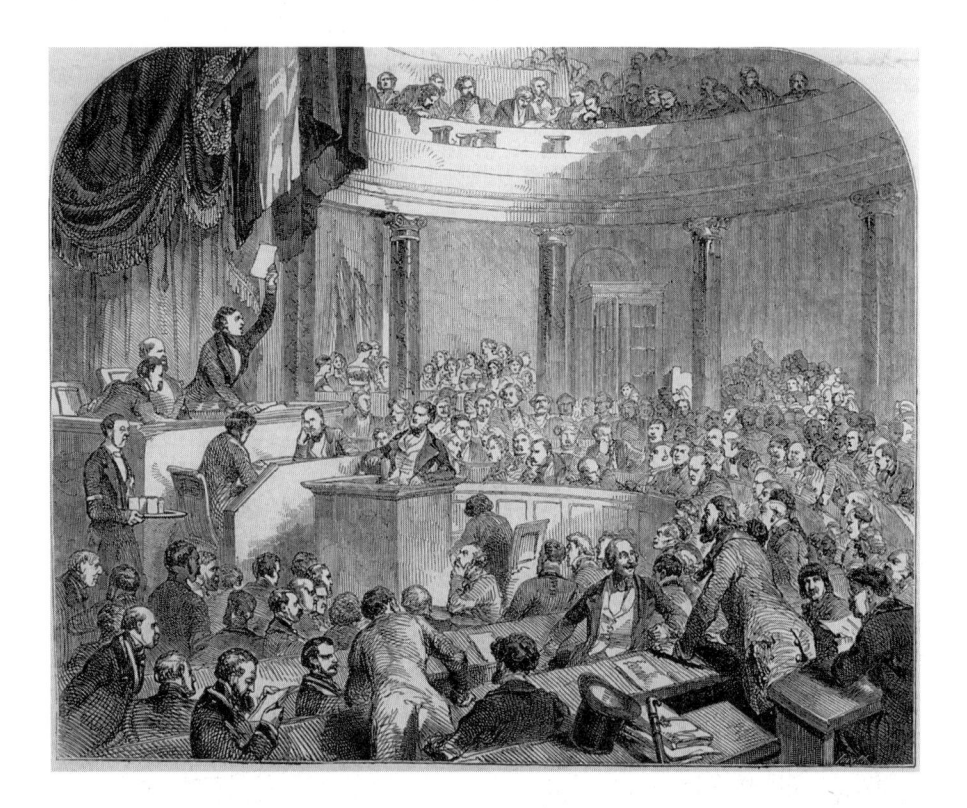

M The *Grossdeutschland–Kleindeutschland* debate – the President of the Frankfurt Parliament (Heinrich von Gägern) speaking on 26 October 1848

I believe, therefore, ... that we must seek a relationship which would not force Austria to detach its German from its non-German provinces, but would keep it in the most intimate association with Germany. The question is therefore: is it more in the interest of Germany that the whole of Germany should only so organise itself, only engage in so lax a unity, that Austria, without being forced to break up the union of its German and non-German provinces in one state, could belong to the *Reich* on the same terms as the other German states? Or is it not in the general interests of the nation of Austria as well as of the rest of Germany, that at least the rest of Germany should form a closer connection; even if Austria because of its non-German provinces cannot enter into this narrowest union on the same terms but that nevertheless a close federal relationship be maintained between Austria and the rest of Germany? ... I have, therefore, in accordance with this view, formulated a motion which I am honoured to announce to the High Assembly: 'In view of its constitutional connection with non-German territories and provinces, Austria remains in permanent and indissoluble union with the rest of Germany. The organic stipulation for this federal relationship made necessary by the changed circumstances will be contained in a special federal act ...'

From M. Gorman: *The Unification of Germany* (1989)

N The vote to exclude the Habsburg Empire from the new Germany taken in the Frankfurt Parliament in 1849

By region	Yes	No	Abstained	Absent	Total
Prussia	150	30	0	17	197
North Germany (excluding Prussia)	72	37	0	14	123
South Germany	39	69	0	19	127
Habsburg Empire	0	88	3	20	111
Total	261	224	3	70	558

From F. Eyck: *The Frankfurt Parliament 1848–1849* (1968)

O A sociologist, writing in the 1850s, comments on the conservative German peasantry

There is an unconquerable conservative force within the German people, a hard core withstands all change, and that is our peasantry. It is truly a unique social class, and no other nation can offer a pendant to it. The man of education may be inclined to conservatism by his understanding, but the peasant is conservative as a matter of habit. In the social conflicts of our time the peasant has played a more important part than most of us realise, for he has formed a natural barrier against the growth of French revolutionary doctrines among the lower classes of society. Only the stolidity of the peasants saved the German thrones in March, 1848. We are told that the revolution stopped short of the thrones. Yet this is not entirely true, for it was the peasants who stopped short of the thrones.

From T.S. Hamerow: *Restoration, Revolution, Reaction* (1966)

P The rejection of the throne of Germany by Frederick William IV in the spring of 1849

Gentlemen, the message you bring me has deeply moved me. It has directed my gaze to the King of Kings, and to the sacred and august duties I have, as the King of my people, and a Prince among the mightiest in Germany. A look in that direction, gentlemen, gives clearness to the vision and certainty to the heart. In the resolution of the German National Assembly you have communicated to me, I recognise the voice of the representatives of the German people. Your call gives me a right, the value of which I know how to prize. If accepted, it demands from me incalculable sacrifices, and burdens me with heavy duties. The German National Assembly has counted on me in all things which were calculated to establish the unity of Germany and the power of Prussia. I honour its confidence; please express my thanks for it. I am ready by deeds to prove that their reliance on my loyalty, love and devotion to the cause of the German Fatherland has not been misplaced. But I should not justify that confidence – I should not answer to the expectations of the German people – I should not strengthen the unity of Germany – if I, violating sacred rights and breaking my former explicit and solemn promises, were, without the voluntary assent of the crowned Princes and free States of our Fatherland, to take a resolution which must be of decisive importance to them and to the States which they rule. It will now lie with the several Governments of the German States to examine together the constitution which the National Assembly has drawn up, and declare whether it will be of advantage to each and to all – whether the rights it confers on me will place me in the position to guide with a strong hand, as my position requires, the destinies of Germany and the great German Fatherland, and realise the expectations of the people. But of this, Germany may be certain, and you may declare it in every State – that if it needs the protection of the Prussian sword or shield from external or internal enemies, I will not fail, even without a summons. I shall follow that course from which my royal House and my people have never departed – the course of Germany loyalty.

From M. Gorman: *The Unification of Germany* (1989)

Q The importance of property rights expressed in a speech to the Frankfurt Parliament in 1848

If you do not respect property in one instance, then you will see that those for whose benefit you committed the violation are also not respected. The propertyless, who are the more numerous than the propertied, will lose the last vestiges of regard for ownership. They will no longer treat with consideration those goods which others acquired through injustice. Remember that respect for property is the basis of all civilisation, and the banner of justice must be raised side by side with the banner of freedom.

From T.S. Hamerow: *Restoration, Revolution, Reaction* (1966)

R The attitude of Frederick William IV, in the view of a modern German writer

Bearing in mind his views it was inevitable that he should decline the German imperial crown offered him by the Frankfurt National Assembly in April 1849. To accept it would have meant placing himself at the head of the German revolution – moreover, when he had only just crushed the revolution in Prussia. Nothing could be further from his mind. But German unity, and under Prussian leadership – that he wanted too; except that this was to be an anti-revolutionary and not a revolutionary unity. In the spring of 1848 his plan had been for a federation of princes to anticipate the German revolution; a year later such a federation was to put an end to the revolution just as the imposed constitution had put an end to it in Prussia.

From Sebastian Haffner: *The Rise and Fall of Prussia* (1980)

S Karl Marx comments on the failure of the 1848 revolution

Thus vanished the German Parliament, and with it the first and last creation of the Revolution. Its convocation had been the first evidence that there actually *had been* a revolution in January; and it existed as long as this, the first modern German Revolution, was not yet brought to a close. Chosen under the influence of the capitalist class by a dismembered, scattered, rural population, for the most part only awaking from the dumbness of feudalism, this Parliament served to bring in one body upon the political arena all the great popular names of 1820–48, and then to utterly ruin them. All the celebrities of middle-class liberalism were here collected. The bourgeoisie expected wonders; it earned shame for itself and its representatives. The industrial and commercial capitalist classes were more severely defeated in Germany than in any other country; they were first worsted, broken, expelled from office in every individual state of Germany, and then put to rout, disgraced and hooted in the Central German Parliament. Political liberalism, the rule of the bourgeoisie, be it under a monarchical or republican form of government, is forever impossible in Germany.

In the latter period of its existence, the German Parliament served to disgrace forever that section which had ever since March 1848 headed the official opposition, the Democrats representing the interests of the small-trading, and partially of the farming class. That class was, in May and June 1849, given a chance to show its means of forming a stable Government in Germany. We have seen how it failed; not so much by adverse circumstances as by the actual and continued cowardice in all trying movements that had occurred since the outbreak of the revolution; by showing in politics the same short-sighted, pusillanimous, wavering spirit, which is characteristic of its commercial operations. In May 1849 it had, by this course, lost the confidence of the real fighting mass of all European insurrections, the working class. But yet, it had a fair chance. The German Parliament belonged to it, exclusively, after the Reactionists and Liberals had withdrawn. The rural population was in its favour. Two-thirds of the armies of the smaller states, one-third of the Prussian army, the majority of the Prussian *Landwehr* [reserve or militia], were ready to join it, if it only acted resolutely, and with that courage which is the result of a clear insight into the state of things. But the politicians who led on this class were not more clear-sighted than the host of petty tradesmen which followed them. They proved even to be more infatuated, more ardently attached to delusions voluntarily kept up, more credulous, more incapable of resolutely dealing with facts than the Liberals. Their political importance, too, is reduced below the freezing-point. But not having actually carried their common-place principles into execution, they were, under *very* favourable circumstances, capable of a momentary resurrection, when this last hope was taken from them, just as it was from their colleagues of the 'pure democracy' in France by the *coup d'état* of Louis Bonaparte.

From M. Gorman: *The Unification of Germany* (1989)

T A modern historian's interpretation of the role of class in the 1848 revolution

The German revolution was determined by political, not by social or economic factors. Although there was some localised social unrest in the forties it did not produce the events of March 1848. The middle classes rose against the absolutism of the princes which seemed to them out of date. Shortly after the event the revolution was rightly called the bourgeois revolution: more recently it has become known as the 'revolution of the intellectuals'. That expression, too, is apposite because professors and writers played an important role both in preparing the revolt and in the Paulskirche [the meeting place of the Frankfurt Parliament]. Only when the revolution was under way did a number of distinct opposition groups develop: the democrats parted company with the liberals and were in turn left by a group which might be described as radical republicans or social democrats.

But one must not think in terms of a great proletarian party such as developed towards the end of the century. There was not the slightest possibility of anything on that scale in Germany in 1848. There were still far more craftsmen and factory workers together. Of these there were not more than a million at the most and many of them still regarded themselves as craftsmen and regretted losing the security and status that went with the craftsman's position.

The workers' congresses which met in Berlin and Frankfurt in 1848 did not discuss the dictatorship of the proletariat but matters of direct concern: the protection of handicrafts, of apprentices and journeymen, the promotion of small-scale industry through patent legislation, export subsidies, cheap imports of raw materials, and also free education, progressive income tax, the welfare of the old and so on.

From Golo Mann: *A History of Germany since 1789* (1974)

U In the view of a modern historian the middle classes failed to grasp the nettle of revolution

On the ruins of the mass insurrection of the March days the middle class prepared to erect the edifice of constitutionalism. The palm of victory went not to the street agitator and barricade warrior but to the parliamentary representative and government bureaucrat ... Without realising, the March ministries deprived themselves of a valuable asset when they suppressed the spring uprising. True they could not afford to ignore the danger of a new proletarian rebellion, but by acting against it with such unrelenting thoroughness they destroyed the insurrectionary élan of the masses once and for all. By the time the parliamentarians prepared to gather the spoils of victory, the Revolution was finished, and the middle class stood isolated.

From T.S. Hamerow: *Restoration, Revolution, Reaction* (1966)

Questions

1. How far do Sources A, B, C, D and E explain the causes of the 1848 revolutions? **(12 marks)**
2. Using Sources F, G and R and your own knowledge, explain why King Frederick William IV placed himself at the head of the German national movement in the spring of 1848. **(8 marks)**
3. What does Source H reveal concerning the importance of the Frankfurt Parliament to the German population? **(4 marks)**
4. What evidence does Source I provide of the disillusionment with the liberal government in Prussia in the spring of 1848? **(4 marks)**
5. How far do Sources J, K and L explain why the majority of Frankfurt parliamentarians were determined to preserve the monarchy? **(8 marks)**
6. Do Sources M, N, P and Q provide a complete explanation for the failure of the Frankfurt Parliament to provide a constitution for a united Germany? **(10 marks)**
7. How far do Sources S, T and U explain the failure of the 1848 revolution in Germany in social terms? **(10 marks)**

2 THE GERMAN CONFEDERATION 1849-62

After the failure of the Frankfurt Parliament to create a united Germany, Frederick William IV of Prussia, advised by his foreign minister Radowitz, attempted to construct a Prussian-dominated German union with the consent of the German princes [A]. A parliament of this proposed union met at Erfurt in March 1850.

However, by this date the power of the Habsburgs had been fully restored in the Austrian Empire and Schwarzenberg, the new Austrian Chancellor, proposed the re-establishment of the old Federal Diet in Frankfurt. For a period in 1850, as the Habsburg Empire re-asserted control in the German Confederation, it seemed there might be war between Austria and Prussia. This was prevented when Prussia bowed to Austrian pressure, the Austrians enjoying the support of Nicholas I of Russia. In November 1850, the new Prussian foreign minister Manteuffel signed an agreement with Schwarzenberg at Olmütz by which Prussia abandoned the Erfurt Union and agreed to a renewed German Confederation [B and C]. Prussia had suffered a considerable political setback but thanks to the Customs Union (*Zollverein*) it enjoyed a strong economic position in Germany [D and E]. The Prussian Customs Union had been established in 1818 and from the early 1820s other German states, recognising its economic benefits, began to join. By the 1850s virtually all the states in the Confederation, except Austria, were members.

The importance of the *Zollverein* was clearly recognised by the Austrians [F], who made every effort to join when the renewal of the organisation was discussed in 1852. This application was resisted by Prussia and when the treaty of renewal for twelve years was signed the Austrian Empire was excluded, which represented a considerable victory for the Prussian kingdom.

In Prussia itself a revised constitution, with a three-class electoral system, was introduced in January 1850 [G]. This lasted without change until 1918. Although the lower classes enjoyed only limited political power, efforts were made to improve their material position [H and I]. At the same time the Prussian economy was growing rapidly [J] so that the basis for Prussian domination of Germany had been prepared even before Bismarck came to power.

A   Radowitz's plan of May 1849 for Prussian domination of Germany
The Governments of Prussia, Saxony and Hanover have concluded the following treaty:

1. The Royal Governments of Prussia, Saxony and Hanover conclude, in compliance with Article 11 of the German Act of Confederation of 8 June 1815, an Alliance with the purpose of safeguarding the internal and external security of Germany and the independence and inviolability of the several German States . . .
2. All members of the German Confederation may join this Alliance . . .
3. (1) The supreme direction of the measures which are to be taken to achieve the aims of the Alliance is vested in the Crown of Prussia . . .
    (2) An Administrative Council, to which all members shall send one or more representatives, shall be formed to conduct the business of the Alliance.
    (3) The Administrative Council may take a final decision on the following matters:
        (i) The admission of new members to the Alliance.
        (ii) Steps for the calling of a constituent *Reichstag* and the direction of its deliberations.
        (iii) The appointment and direction of civil commissioners to be attached to the military when requests for assistance against internal disturbances are made.
4. Should there be diplomatic negotiations . . . they shall be conducted by the Crown of Prussia, and the Administrative Council shall be kept informed of their progress . . .

From L.L. Snyder (ed.): *Documents of German History* (1958)

B The effects of the Olmütz Agreement on Prussia
(i) Manteuffel speaks to the Prussian Parliament in December 1850
The strong man may retreat a step but he keeps his gaze fixed firmly on the goal and decides in what other way he can achieve it.

(ii) Prince William of Prussia, 1850
Confidence in the strength and goodwill of Prussia, or rather in its *savoir-faire*, has been shaken for a long time to come.

From T.S. Hamerow: *Restoration, Revolution, Reaction* (1966)

C The effect of the Olmütz Agreement of Germany, as perceived by Bernhard von Bülow, *Reich* Chancellor 1900–1909
True the national movement in favour of unity had been placed on a solid foundation by the Prussian tariff policy, but the conference of Olmütz shattered the hopes of German patriots who looked to Prussia for a fulfilment of their wishes as a nation. Prussia seemed to renounce her mission of a world-wide importance, and to relinquish the policy,

worthy of a Great Power, of carrying on the work of unification – work she had begun with a definite politico-economical objective.

From Bernhard von Bülow: *Imperial Germany* (1914)

D Two contemporary assessments of the significance of the *Zollverein*

(i) John Bowring, a British manufacturer, reporting in 1840
The general feeling in Germany towards the *Zollverein* is that it is the first step in what is called the Germanisation of the country ... By a community of interest in commercial and trading questions it has prepared the way for political nationality.

(ii) Metternich, writing in 1833
The situation has changed as a result of the Prussian Customs Union. Now a number of independent states accept, in relation to a neighbouring superior power, the obligation of conforming to *its* laws, or submitting to *its* administrative measures and *its* control in a most important branch of public finance. Little by little, under the direction of Prussian and by the necessary formation of common interests, the states which make up the union will compose a more or less compact body, which in every matter (and not simply in commercial affairs) will act and vote in common on the basis of pre-arranged principles. Prussia can be counted upon to utilise all the resources of her political activity.

From M. Gorman: *The Unification of Germany* (1989)

E The proposals of Baron von Bruck, the Austrian Minister of Commerce, for a Central European Customs Union

Austria has, above all, one thing to prevent, namely that the *Zollverein*, due to expire at the end of 1852, should be renewed before the Austro-German Customs Union is irrevocably settled on a sure foundation. Such a renewal would bind all the German states for twelve years longer to Prussia's will in all national economic affairs. If Prussia were to see her supremacy assured for so long a time, she would scarcely be persuaded to enter the Customs Union with Austria – even though it offered the most convincing economic advantages – and to share, to that degree, her supremacy with her. The matter would, however, stand quite differently if the renewal of the *Zollverein* were put in question by several of its members, or if it were made dependent upon the previous achievement of a Customs Union with Austria; for rather than endanger the intellectual and economic supremacy that she gained through the *Zollverein*, Prussia would prefer an attempt to share it with Austria ...

The advantages that Germany might expect from such Customs Union would be: the moral unity which the same tariff and commercial laws, the common administration of these affairs, and an unobstructed internal economy would stimulate; closer political links; a large market; complementary industries in the various states, strengthening and stimulating each other, greater power and still greater standing abroad; the multiplication of shipping routes and a most remunerative overseas trade; finally, the satisfaction of the just wishes and expectations of the nation, to whom would be assured all the advantages of German unity without the dangerous disadvantages to particularist interests. Perhaps one might also mention that Austria herself, notwithstanding the political differences still outstanding, unreservedly offers her hand to help forward this unity, because she does not wish to withhold these advantages from the nation any longer and because she hopes to succeed through this unity in settling agitation on other matters . . .

From M. Gorman: *The Unification of Germany* (1989)

F   The significance of the Prussian constitution, as seen by a modern historian

The distribution of power in Prussia was such that the Minorities, the civil servants, the army, the landowners and above all the dynasty, which had always regarded the Prussian state as its property, were able to exert an influence not provided for in the constitution and entirely unrelated to the numerical or economic importance of these groups.

From Golo Mann: *A History of Germany since 1789* (1974)

The German Confederation 1849–62

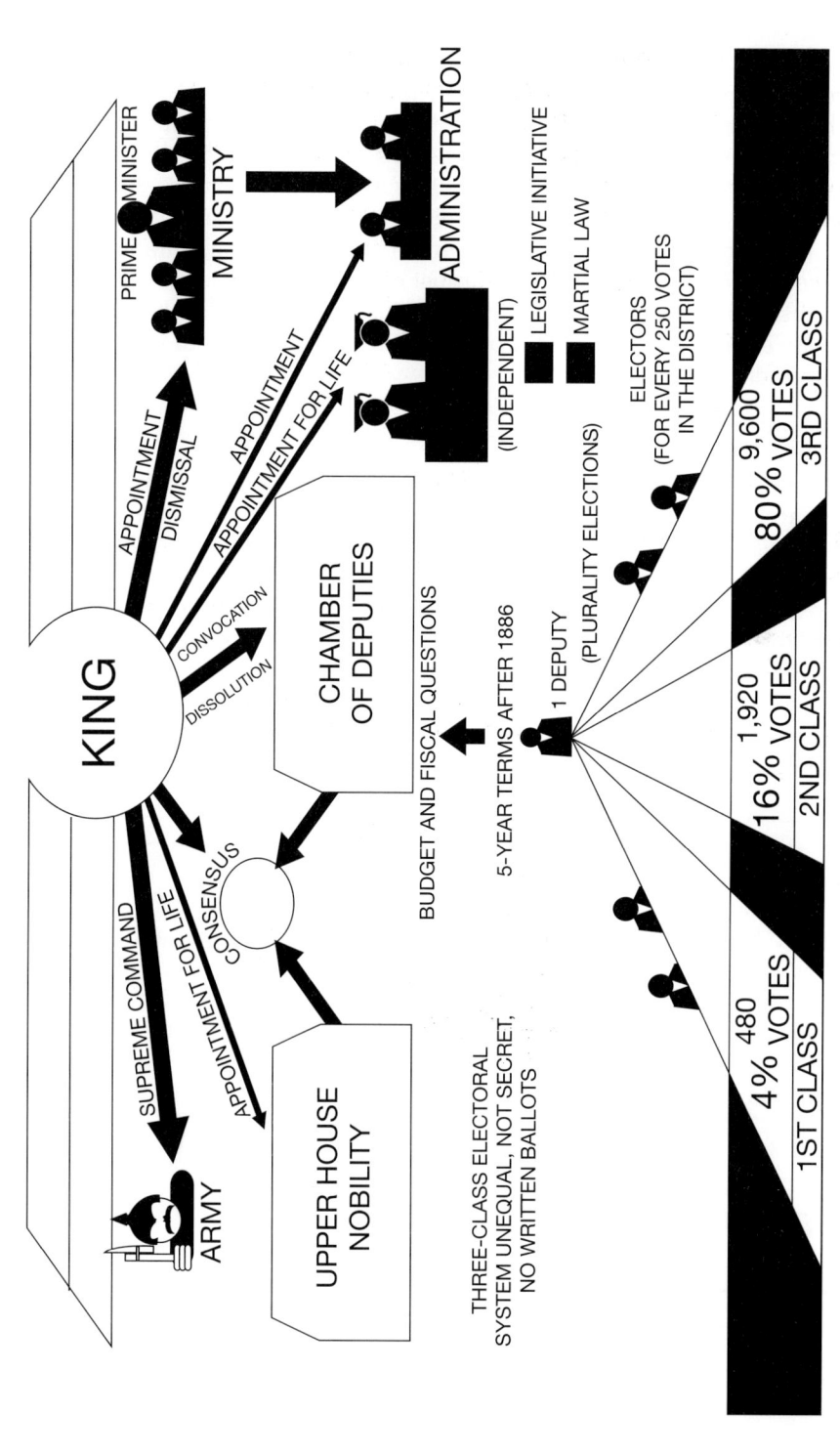

G The Revised Prussian Constitution, 31 January 1850

H The need for social welfare – from Leopold von Ranke's Memorandum to Frederick William IV, 1850

For he who serves the state with his life has also a claim on it for his support. The soundest policy would be to satisfy this claim, since as a matter of fact it is dangerous to train year after year the entire youthful population in the use of arms, and then alienate a large and physically perhaps the most vigorous part, leaving it exposed to the agitation of the enemies of all order. Either we must exempt the propertyless from duty to serve in the army, or we must place them under an obligation to the state even after their period of service by the prospect of gainful employment.

From T.S. Hamerow: *Restoration, Revolution, Reaction* (1966)

I The position of the artisan as expressed by Bismarck in 1849

The shareholder in railroads demands a guarantee of his dividends, the industrialist, the mineowner, the shipper, the viniculturist etc., they all demand to be protected in their occupations by tariff laws at the expense of their customers. Why do you not want to grant this favour as well to the more numerous and more moderate class, the artisan class? Factories enrich the individual but they also breed proletarians, a mass of undernourished workers who are a menace to the state because of the insecurity of their livelihood. Handicraftsmen, on the other hand, constitute the backbone of the burgher class.

From T.S. Hamerow: *Restoration, Revolution, Reaction* (1966)

J A modern analysis of the economic growth of Prussia

By an accident of geography German industrial expansion occurred largely in Prussian territory in the Ruhr, Silesia and the Saarland – Saxony was the only significant exception. Consequently the economic balance of power was moving slowly in favour of Prussia in Germany and in Europe throughout the 1850s and 1860s; long before the battles of Sadowa and Sedan were fought. Prussia had drawn ahead of Austria and France in the industrial race.

From William Carr: *A History of Germany 1815–1990* (1991)

Questions

1. Using Sources A, B and C, show in what ways the Olmütz agreement affected the ambitions of Prussia's political leaders. **(8 marks)**
2. Using the evidence in Sources D and E, explain how the *Zollverein* influenced the growth of Prussian power within the German confederation. **(5 marks)**

The German Confederation 1849–62

3 In what ways do Sources F and G indicate that the Prussian constitution was not fully democratic? **(8 marks)**

4 Using Sources H and I and your own knowledge, explain why the Prussian government was so concerned with the condition of the lower classes in Prussian society. **(8 marks)**

5 Does Source J support the view that Prussia would have dominated a united German empire even if Bismarck's policies had not been applied? **(4 marks)**

3 THE RISE OF BISMARCK

Otto von Bismarck was born into a Junker family at Schönhausen just east of the Elbe on 1 April 1815. He moved to Berlin when he was seven, went to the best Berlin grammar school and, afterwards, to the University of Göttingen. According to his memoirs he had already formed many of his political ideas by this time [A].

In May 1835 he scraped through the examination which qualified him for entry into the Prussian civil service. He served for a short time in Aachen followed by a year's military service and then resigned from the Prussian bureaucracy in 1839. For the next eight years he lived as a Prussian landowner, a period of his life which apparently he found very boring.

In 1847 he became a member of the Prussian United Diet but only as a substitute when an elected member became ill. In the Diet he opposed every liberal proposal and by the end of the session had achieved a reputation as an extreme reactionary. When the 1848 revolution broke out in Berlin, Bismarck tried unsuccessfully to persuade the Prussian generals to stage a counter-revolution. He was then elected to the Prussian Parliament when King Frederick William IV introduced a new constitution. In December 1850 he defended the peace achieved by the Olmütz agreement in the Parliament [B].

Bismarck was appointed by the King to be the Prussian representative to the restored German Confederation (*Bund*), taking up his appointment in May 1851 [C]. For the next eight years he aimed to achieve Prussian domination of the Confederation by diplomacy. He had little respect for the Austrian Empire either as the leader of the German states or as a potential ally [D, E]. However, his views did not prevail since King Frederick William renewed the Austro-Prussian defensive alliance in April 1854. Bismarck made it clear that he would conduct diplomacy only on the basis of his perception of Prussian interests [F]. In a memorandum which he wrote to Prince William in March 1858 he made his views very strongly known [G].

Prince William became Regent in 1858 and King in 1861. In 1859 Bismarck moved from Frankfurt when he was sent as ambassador to St Petersburg. While in that position he wrote the Baden-Baden Memorial in October 1861 explaining the possibility of exploiting the *Zollverein* for political purposes [H]. He hoped to achieve a position in the Prussian government, an ambition he did not abandon when he was sent as ambassador to France in March 1862.

The Rise of Bismarck

A   Bismarck recollects his early political lessons (Bismarck's memoirs were written in the aftermath of his loss of the chancellorship and are by no means always reliable.)

My historical sympathies remained on the side of authority ... Every German prince who resisted the Emperor before the Thirty Years' War roused my ire; but from the Great Elector onwards I was partisan enough to take an anti-imperial view, and to find it natural that things should have been in readiness for the Seven Years' War. Yet the German-national feeling remained so strong in me that, at the beginning of my university life, I at once entered into relations with the *Burschenschaft*, a group of students which made the promotion of a national sentiment its aim ... In my first half-year at Göttingen occurred the Hambach Festival (27 May 1832), the 'festal ode' of which still remains in my memory; in my third the Frankfurt outbreak (3 April 1833). These manifestations revolted me. Mob interference with political authority conflicted with my Prussian schooling, and I returned to Berlin with less liberal opinions than when I quitted it; but this reaction was again somewhat mitigated when I was brought into immediate connexion with the workings of the political machine. Upon foreign politics, with which the public at that time occupied itself but little, my views, as regards the War of Liberation, were taken from the standpoint of a Prussian officer. On looking at the map, the possession of Strasburg by France exasperated me, and a visit to Heidelberg, Spires and the Palatinate made me feel revengeful and militant ...

From Bismarck: *Reflections and Reminiscences 1891–1898* (1898)

B   Bismarck opposes war in a speech made in the Prussian Parliament in December 1850

... what kind of a war is this? Not an expedition of isolated regiments to Schleswig or Baden, not a military promenade through troubled provinces, but a major war against two of the three great continental powers, whilst the third mobilises on our frontier, eager for conquest and well aware that in Cologne there is treasure to be found which could end the French Revolution and give their rulers the French Imperial crown. A war, gentlemen, which will begin by forcing us to give up some of the remoter Prussian provinces, in which a large part of Prussia will be inundated by enemy forces, and which will bring to our provinces the full horrors of war. A war, it can be assumed, that the Minister of Public Worship, who has jurisdiction over the servants of religion, peace and love, must loathe to the bottom of his heart. [Laughter] A war, which the Minister for Trade and Industry must be convinced will begin by destroying the public welfare entrusted to his care, and which the Finance Minister can only desire when the money can no longer be left in the royal coffers. And yet I would not shrink from such a war, indeed I would advise it, if someone could prove to me that it was necessary, or show me a worthy goal which could only be attained by it and in no other way. Why do large states go to war nowadays? The only sound basis for a large state, and this is what distinguishes it from a small state, is state egoism and not romanticism, and it is not worthy of a great state to fight for something that is not in its own interest. Show me, therefore, gentlemen, an objective worthy of war, and I will agree with you. It is easy for a statesman, whether in the Cabinet or the Chamber, to use the public wind to blow the trumpets of war, and to sit at home by his own fireside or make thundering speeches from the rostrum, and leave it to the musketeer, pouring out his life's blood on the snowy wastes, to decide whether the system will bring glory or victory or no. Nothing is easier, but woe unto the statesman who at this time does not seek a cause for war that will endure when the war is over . . .

From W.N. Medlicott and D.K. Coveney (eds.): *Bismarck and Europe* (1971)

C Bismarck on diplomacy (writing to his wife in May 1851)

In the art of using many words to say nothing at all I am making rapid progress. I write reports of many pages which read neatly and clearly like newspapers leaders, and if Manteuffel [the Prussian Minster-President], when he has read them, can say what is in them, he is cleverer than I am. Each of us behaves as though he thinks the others are brimming over with thoughts and plans, if he could only formulate them, and yet all of us together are not a whit wiser as to what will or should become of Germany. No one, not even the most malevolent sceptic of a democrat, would believe what charlatanry and pomposity there is in this diplomacy . . .

From W.N. Medlicott and D.K. Coveney (eds.): *Bismarck and Europe* (1971)

D Bismarck's views on the Austrian Empire, contained in a letter to Manteuffel, February 1854

I cannot deny that I have been somewhat alarmed to learn from friends' letters that in His Majesty's entourage there is a kind of gloom at the thought of the isolation we should find ourselves in after a breach with Russia, and a feeling that it is essential to seek a closer tie with Austria and avoid all disputes with her. I should be very uneasy if we sought refuge from a possible storm by hitching our trim and seaworthy frigate to that worm-eaten old Austrian man-of-war. Of the two we are the better swimmers and a welcome ally for *anyone*; if we want to give up our possible isolation and strict neutrality it would be difficult just now to avoid the appearance of anxiously seeking for support, whereas later

The Rise of Bismarck

we could lay down conditions in return for our aid. Great crises produce the weather conditions which promote the growth of Prussia, and we have used them fearlessly, even ruthlessly. If we want to make further growth, then at least we must not be afraid to stand alone with [our] 400 000 men, particularly while the other powers are fighting each other and thus we, by taking sides with each of them, can make a better bargain than by an early and unconditional alliance with such an ineffective fighter and insincere partner as Austria.

From W.N. Medlicott and D.K. Coveney (eds.): *Bismarck and Europe* (1971)

E A modern historian's interpretation of Bismarck's attitude to the Austrian Empire

It would be rash to conclude ... that Bismarck had no principles or that he had abandoned the cause of conservatism. He always concentrated on the task in hand and, when he was following a trail, he would reject every scent that led away from it. Conflict with Austria was the only thing that mattered to him during his years at Frankfurt; he judged all international affairs from this angle ... Moreover Bismarck had grown up when Prussia was the least of the great powers; the memories of the Napoleonic wars were always at the back of his mind. He underrated Prussian strength and overrated that of others.

From A.J.P. Taylor: *Bismarck, the Man and the Statesman* (1955)

F Prussia and the Confederation – Bismarck writing in May 1857

Usefulness for the Confederation should not be the exclusive guideline for Prussian policy, for the most useful thing for the *Bund* would be, without any doubt at all, to subordinate ourselves and all the German governments, militarily, politically and commercially, under Austria in the *Zollverein*; under united leadership the *Bund* could achieve other things in peace and war, and would be in a strong defensive position in case of war. I only mention this in order to show that the consolidation of Austria's military position in South Germany cannot be a matter of complete indifference, even if it is advantageous to the *Bund*, particularly from Austria's point of view.

From W.N. Medlicott and D.K. Coveney (eds.): *Bismarck and Europe* (1971)

G Bismarck's advice to Prince William in March 1858

The position of Prussia would perhaps be better if the *Bund* did not exist; the closer relations with neighbours which Prussia needs would have been brought about, and under Prussia's leadership. But seeing that it does exist, and the misuse of its institutions against Prussia has some prospect of success, Prussia's task can only be to fulfil faithfully all its indubitable obligations to the *Bund* in peace and war, but to curtail at the expense of the independence of the various members any development of the power of the *Bund* which goes beyond the strict letter of the treaty. By doing this Prussia would not be in any way unfaithful to her German ideals, she would only be resisting the pressure of a conception, invented by her opponents, that *'Bundestag'* and *'Deutschland'* are identical, and that Prussia's German-mindedness should be judged according to the extent of her submission to the majority of the *Bund* members. No state has the urge and opportunity to assert its German point of view independently of the *Bund* assembly to the same extent as Prussia, and it may at the same time prove that Prussia is of more importance to the middle and smaller states than a majority of nine votes for Prussia. Prussian interests coincide exactly with those of most of the *Bund countries* except Austria, but not with those of the *Bund governments*, and there is nothing more German than the development of Prussia's particular interests, properly understood...

From W.N. Medlicott and D.K. Coveney (eds.): *Bismarck and Europe* (1971)

H Bismarck's Baden-Baden Memorial, written July–October 1861

The practical realisation of a German national representation has so far not been possible by federal constitutional means, and could only go hand in hand with a complete overhaul of the central government. But it might be a less hopeless task to set up other national arrangements in the same way that the *Zollverein* was created.

Whether and how the *Zollverein* can be renewed after completion of its present term, only time can decide. It is, however, desirable that it should not continue in its present form, under which the right of veto of the various members can hinder the development of our commercial legislation. Here, too, besides introducing the right to pass resolutions on at least a two-thirds majority, further difficulties could most easily be solved by committees of varying numbers from the Estate assemblies of the various states, who by consulting together would try and settle the differences of opinion amongst the governments. Such a *'Zollparlament'* could, under certain circumstances and with skilful leadership, pave the way for agreements in other spheres into which German states would more likely be prepared to enter if they always remained terminable on the giving of notice...

From W.N. Medlicott and D.K. Coveney (eds.): *Bismarck and Europe* (1971)

The Rise of Bismarck

Questions

1 What light does Source A throw on the formation of Bismarck's political ideas? **(6 marks)**
2 Using your own knowledge, and Source B, explain Bismarck's attitude to war. **(9 marks)**
3 How far do Sources C, D and E show Bismarck as an exponent of *Realpolitik?* **(9 marks)**
4 What indications do Sources F and G give of Bismarck's attitude to the German Confederation? **(7 marks)**
5 What does Source H tell us about Bismarck's attitude to a *Zollparlament?* **(5 marks)**

4 BISMARCK AND PRUSSIAN DOMINATION IN GERMANY 1862–71

In September 1862 William I fell into dispute with the moderate liberal majority in the Prussian Parliament over the military budget. In desperation, after considering abdication, he appointed Bismarck Minister-President and Foreign Minister of Prussia. Bismarck stated that he saw this dispute as involving the ultimate power of the monarchy [A].

He had the objective of establishing Prussian domination in Germany and he made clear in a speech to the budget committee, very much criticised at the time, that a successful foreign policy would be based on Prussian military power [B]. In reality his methods were those of a successful pragmatist, exploiting opportunities as they occurred and being prepared to use the power of the Prussian army only if all else failed.

In the autumn of 1863, by persuading William I not to attend a meeting of German rulers at Frankfurt, he outmanoeuvred the Austrian government which was proposing to restructure the German Confederation [C]. In the same year, following a nationalist revolt in the Polish provinces of the Russian Empire, he signed the Alvensleben Convention with Russia, cementing good relations between the two powers [D].

In November 1863 Christian IX of Denmark ratified a new Danish constitution incorporating the Duchy of Schleswig into his kingdom. This infringed the 1852 Treaty of London and provided Bismarck with a chance to act and eventually make Schleswig, Holstein and Lauenburg part of the kingdom of Prussia [E]. As a first step, he signed a joint agreement with Austria that the two powers would set aside the new Danish constitution and themselves decide the future of the duchies. The Danish army was defeated by the Austro-Prussian forces in 1864, and under the terms of the Treaty of Verona, October 1864, the territories were to be jointly administered. Afterwards Austria proposed that the duchies should be ruled by the German claimant, the Duke of Augustenburg, but this was rejected by Bismarck. Instead, by the Convention of Gastein, Prussia was to rule Schleswig and Austria to rule Holstein [F].

Napoleon III was alarmed by this apparent Austro-Prussian reconciliation, which he identified as potentially dangerous to France. However, Bismarck was able to reassure him in a meeting at Biarritz [G]. Having secured his relations with France, Bismarck increasingly faced Austria with the prospect of war if she was not prepared to hand over the duchies completely to Prussia. In April 1866 he signed a treaty with the

Bismarck and Prussian Domination in Germany 1862–71

Italian government agreeing to join a war of alliance with Prussia against the Austrian Empire to secure Venetia, providing it occurred within three months.

Bismarck used every effort to make Austria appear as the aggressor but even when Prussian forces invaded Holstein in June 1866 the Austrian troops withdrew without fighting. Consequently, on 18 June Prussia declared war. Although most of the German states joined the Austrians they were defeated at the battle of Königgrätz at the beginning of July. Bismarck then had to restrain William I and the Prussian generals who wanted to carry the war into the heart of the Austrian Empire [H].

The Peace of Prague, signed on 27 August 1866, dissolved the German Confederation and gave Prussia control of Germany north of the River Main through the newly established North German Confederation. Napoleon III demanded compensation for this increase in Prussian power but his claims were rejected [I, J].

In the aftermath of the Austro-Prussian war Bismarck's first priority was the consolidation of the North German Confederation, and it is not clear when he determined to take over the South German states. Nevertheless, even without the further expansion of Prussian power he considered war with France likely in the near future [K]. In the event, the offer of the Spanish throne to Prince Leopold of Hohenzollern-Sigmaringen in 1869, although initially declined, worsened Franco-Prussian relations. When the offer was renewed, Leopold under pressure from Bismarck, and against the wishes of William I, reluctantly accepted [L].

A German prince on the throne of Spain was seen as threatening the southern frontier of France and there was a consequent storm of protest in France. The French ambassador, Benedetti, was sent to Ems to persuade William I to forbid Leopold's acceptance of the offer, something the King had already prohibited. However, when Benedetti attempted to gain an assurance that the canditature of Leopold would not be renewed, William refused and sent a telegram to Bismarck announcing his decision. A version of this, suitably edited by Bismarck, was published – the infamous Ems telegram [M]. In his memoirs Bismarck claimed that it was the telegram that pushed France into declaring war.

The outcome of the Franco-Prussian war, 1870–71, was the defeat of France and the entry of the South German states into the German Empire [N]. However, it was only with difficulty that William I was persuaded to become German Emperor. At the same time the seeds of future conflict with France were sown in the Peace of Frankfurt, ending the Franco-Prussian war in 1871, when Germany acquired most of Alsace and Lorraine [O, P].

A Bismarck's account of his appointment by William I

The King invited me to accompany him into the park ... I succeeded in convincing him that, so far as he was concerned, it was not a question of Liberal or Conservative of this or that shade, but rather monarchical rule or parliamentary government, and that the latter must be avoided at all costs, if even by a period of dictatorship. I said, 'In this situation I shall, even if your Majesty command me to do things which I do not consider right, tell you my opinion quite openly, but if you finally persist in yours, I will rather perish with the King than forsake your Majesty in the contest with parliamentary government.' This view was at that time strong and absolute in me, because I regarded the negations and phrases of the Opposition of that day as politically disastrous in face of the national task of Prussia, and because I cherished such strong feelings of devotion and affection for William I, that the thought of perishing with him appeared to me, under the circumstances, a natural and congenial conclusion to my life.

From Bismarck: *Reflections and Reminiscences 1891–1898* (1898)

B Bismarck states his priorities (in a speech made to the Prussian budget committee, 1862)

We are perhaps too 'educated' to put up with a constitution; we are too critical; the ability to judge government measures and bills of the National Assembly is too widespread; there are in the country too many subversive elements who have an interest in revolutionary change. This may sound paradoxical, but it goes to show how difficult it is in Prussia to carry on a constitutional existence ... We are too ardent, we like to carry too heavy a weight of armour for our fragile bodies; but we should also make use of it. Germany doesn't look to Prussian liberalism, but to its power: Bavaria, Württemberg, Baden can indulge in liberalism, but no one will expect them to undertake Prussia's role. Prussia must gather and consolidate her strength in readiness for the favourable moment, which has already been missed several times. Prussia's boundaries according to the Vienna treaties are not favourable to a healthy political life; not by means of speeches and majority verdicts will the great decisions of the time be made – that was the great mistake of 1848 and 1849 – but by iron and blood ...

From W.N. Medlicott and D.K. Coveney (eds.): *Bismarck and Europe* (1971)

C Bismarck persuades William I not to attend the meeting at Frankfurt

On the return journey from Baden-Baden to Berlin 31 August the King passed so near to Frankfurt that his decision not to take part in the Congress became known to every one. The majority, or at least the most powerful, of the princes felt very uncomfortable at this time when they thought of the scheme of reform which, if Prussia held aloof, left him standing alone with Austria in a connection where they got no protection from the rivalry of the two Great Powers. The Vienna Cabinet must have thought of the possibility that the other Federal princes would agree in the Congress to the proposals made on 17 August, even when they had been finally left alone with Austria in the reformed federal relation. Otherwise it would not have been demanded of the princes who remained at Frankfurt that they should accept the Austrian proposals and carry them into practice without the consent of Prussia. But at Frankfurt the middle states did not desire either a solely Prussian or a solely Austrian leadership; they wanted to hold as influential a position as arbiters in the sense of the Triad, by which each of the two Great Powers would be driven to compete for the votes of the middle states. To demand of Austria that they should conclude without Prussia they replied by referring to the necessity of fresh negotiations with Prussia and by announcing their own inclination to such a course.

The form of their reply to the wishes of Austria was not smooth enough not to excite some irritation at Vienna. The effect on Count Rechberg [Austrian foreign minister], prepared by the friendly relations in which our acting as colleagues at Frankfurt had ended, was to make him say that the road to Berlin was not longer or more difficult for Austria than for the middle states.

From Bismarck: *Reflections and Reminiscences 1891–1898* (1898)

D Bismarck cements relations with Russia (from the text of the Alvensleben Convention, February 1863)

The two courts of Russia and Prussia, recognising that the events which have unexpectedly taken place in the kingdom of Poland constitute a serious threat to public and private *property* and may also affect the interests of public order, commerce and industry in the neighbouring Prussian provinces, have agreed:

That on the demand of the Commander in Chief of the Russian army in the kingdom of Poland or of General of Infantry Werder, commanding the first, second, fifth and sixth Prussian army corps, or of the neighbouring authorities of the two countries, the commanders of Russian and Prussian detachments shall be authorised to hold themselves ready for mutual cooperation, and in case of need to cross the border in order to pursue the rebels who pass from one country to another. Special officers shall be sent by both sides, for service in the headquarters of the two armies and with the commanding officers of the detachments, with a view to the practical execution of this agreement. These officers will be kept informed of any military redeployment so as to be able to communicate them to their respective commanding officers.

Secret article:
It has been agreed with Prince Gortschakov [Russian chancellor and

foreign minister] that any signs of political intrigues relating to the Grand Duchy of Posen shall be transmitted by him directly to Berlin and communicated by the head of the diplomatic chancellery at Warsaw to the Prussian officer destined to reside in the town, who will pass them on to General Werder.

From W.N. Medlicott and D.K. Coveney (eds.): *Bismarck and Europe* (1971)

E   Bismarck, in a letter to the Prussian representative at Frankfurt in December 1862, gives his views on Schleswig-Holstein

I am certain of this, that the whole Danish business can be settled in a way desirable for us only by war. The occasion for such a war can be found at any moment that we find favourable for waging it. Until then, much more depends on the attitude of the non-German Great Powers towards the affair than on the intrigues of the Würzburg coalition governments and their influence on German sentiment. The disadvantage of having signed the London Protocol [the 1852 Treaty of London] we share with Austria and cannot free ourselves from the consequences of that signature without war. If war comes, however, the future territorial status of Denmark will depend upon its results.

It cannot be foreseen what development of German Federal relations is destined for the future; as long, however, as they remain about the same as in the past, I cannot regard it as in the interest of Prussia to wage a war in order, as the most favourable result, to install in Schleswig-Holstein a new Grand Duke, who in fear of Prussian lust for annexation, will vote against us in the Diet and whose government, in spite of the gratitude due to Prussia for its installation, will be a ready object of Austrian machination . . .

From Bismarck: *Reflections and Reminiscences 1891–1898* (1898)

F   The convention of Gastein, signed between Austria and Prussia in August 1865, increases Prussian influence

Article I. The exercise of the Rights acquired in common by the High Contracting Parties, in virtue of Article III of the Vienna Treaty of Peace of 30th October, 1864, shall, without prejudice to the continuance of those rights of both Powers to the whole of both Duchies, pass to His Majesty the Emperor of Austria as regards the Duchy of Holstein, and to His Majesty the King of Prussia as regards the Duchy of Schleswig. *Article II.* The High Contracting Parties will propose to the Diet the establishment of a German Fleet, and will fix upon the harbour of Kiel as a Federal Harbour for the said Fleet. Until the resolutions of the Diet with respect to this proposal have been carried into effect, the Ships of War of both Powers shall use this Harbour, and the Command and the Police Duties within it shall be exercised by Prussia. Prussia is entitled

both to establish the necessary Fortifications opposite Friedrichsort for the protection of the entrance, and also to fit up along the Holstein bank of the inlet the Naval Establishments that are requisite in a Military Port. These Fortifications and Establishments remain likewise under Prussian command, and the Prussian marines and troops required for their Garrison and Protection may be quartered in Kiel and the neighbourhood.
Article III. The High Contracting Parties will propose in Frankfurt the elevation of Rendsburg into a German Federal Fortress. Until the Diet shall have issued the regulations respecting Garrisoning the said Fortress, the Garrison shall consist of Imperial Austrian and Royal Prussian troops under a command annually alternating on the 1st July.
Article IV. While the division agreed upon in Article I of the present Convention continues, the Royal Prussian Government shall retain two Military Roads through Holstein; the one from Lübeck to Kiel, the other from Hamburg to Rendsburg.

All details as to the Military Stations, and as to the transport and subsistence of the Troops, shall be regulated as soon as possible in a Special Convention. Until this has been done, the Regulations in force as to the Prussian Military Roads through Hanover shall be observed.
Article V. Prussia retains the disposal of one telegraphic wire for communication with Kiel and Rendsburg. She will in due course request the granting of the concession for a railway from Lübeck through Kiel to Schleswig.
Article VI. [The Duchies shall in due course enter the *Zollverein*.]
Article VII. Prussia is entitled to make the Canal that is to be cut between the North Sea and the Baltic, through the territory of Holstein, according to the result of the professional investigations undertaken by the Prussian Government...

From W.N. Medlicott and D.K. Coveney (eds.): *Bismarck and Europe* (1971)

G   Bismarck reports to William I in October 1865 on his meeting with Napoleon III

They had exaggerated in Paris the importance of the Gastein agreement for the general policy of Prussia, especially as they could not believe that a result which was so advantageous to Prussia had not been purchased by some secret concessions to Austria. The Emperor let it be seen that the Austrian communication, which had reached him by very confidential channels (apparently through Her Majesty the Empress), had supported the hypothesis of a secret understanding of the German Powers, directed as a sort of coalition against France. Again His Majesty solemnly put the question to me, whether we had not given Austria some guarantee about Venetia. I denied it... moreover, I thought it impossible that we would conclude an agreement in the future whereby Austria could make a war in which Prussia would have to join without advantage to herself. The Emperor thereupon assured me that he did not intend to initiate any plans which might disturb the peace of Europe ... I emphasised the point that the acquisition of the Elbe Duchies was not itself a strengthening of Prussian power; on the contrary, by deploying our navy and developing our defensive position northwards it would tie up the forces of our Fatherland in more than one direction to an extent which would not be compensated by the addition of a million inhabitants.

From W.N. Medlicott and D.K. Coveney (eds.): *Bismarck and Europe* (1971)

H Bismarck urges peace with Austria (The Nikolsburg Memorandum, 24 July 1866)

Regarding the negotiations with Austria to find a basis for peace, I respectfully beg Your Majesty to allow me to lay before you the following considerations:

It seems to me of the greatest importance that the present favourable moment should not be missed. (William I: Agreed)

By Your Majesty's declared acceptance *en bloc* of the proposals of His Majesty the Emperor of the French, the danger of France's taking sides against Prussia, which by diplomatic pressure could easily turn into active participation, has been eliminated. (William I: Correct)

As a result of the instructions given to Count Goltz [the Prussian ambassador in Paris] on Your Majesty's orders, it has been possible to secure in addition from the Emperor Napoleon the definite assurance, as Count Goltz reported telegraphically on 22 inst., that he will not only allow the direct annexation of four million in N Germany, but will himself recommend it, without any mention being made of compensation for France. (William I: Correct)

But the wavering of the Emperor in the last few weeks, and the pressure of public opinion in France, raise definite fears that, if the present concessions are not quickly converted into fact, then there could be a new *volte-face*. We cannot count on support from the other great powers for further, or even these, Prussian demands. Your Majesty has observed in the letters of HM the Emperor of Russia with what alarm he views the Prussian conditions. His Minister, Prince Gortschakov, has also expressed the wish to know these conditions, both through Your Majesty's ambassador in St Petersburg and Baron Oubril in Berlin. (William I: Russia's proposal for a congress is already evidence of this, for Russia will use this to oppose the peace preliminaries.)

The family connexions of the Russian Imperial house with German dynasties give rise to the fear that in further negotiations sympathy with them will carry great weight. In England, public opinion begins to veer towards Your Majesty's military victories: but the same cannot be said of the government, and it can only be assumed that it will recognise the *faits accomplis*. The double declaration of Austria that it will withdraw from the German *Bund* and agree to a reconstruction of it under Prussia's leadership without Austria's participation, and that it will recognise everything that Your Majesty thinks fit to do in N Germany, provides all the essentials that Prussia demands of her.

From W.N. Medlicott and D.K. Coveney (eds.): *Bismarck and Europe* (1971)

I The French ask for compensation – Bismarck warns Goltz on 5 August 1866

Secret. Benedetti [the French ambassador to Prussia] has just sent the following plan for a secret convention:
1   Prussia gives France the 1814 frontier.
2   Prussia persuades Bavaria and Hesse-Darmstadt to give up all territories on the left bank of the Rhine to France, stipulating indemnities to be paid *by us*.
3   Prussia relinquishes all links with Limburg and Luxemburg, and garrison rights to the latter.

As there is no mention of a *quid pro quo* for Prussia, this is the compensation for our annexations.

This sharply contradicts everything that the Emperor has repeatedly told you. I would never entertain the slightest hope of getting the King's consent to this, but will in any case not propose anything so extensive. I am sending you this preliminary account for your own personal information, without prejudice to a further communication in due course.

From W.N. Medlicott and D.K. Coveney (eds.): *Bismarck and Europe* (1971)

J The French claims are rejected, as Bismarck tells Goltz on 8 August 1866

The Emperor justifies his demands by reference to his country and public opinion: we counter that by referring to our country and our public opinion. We cannot reconcile with the good sense, which we normally admire in him, the making of demands upon us which involve a humiliation of Prussia, and which will inevitably lead to fresh irreconcilable animosity of Prussians and Germans towards France. I repeat the question: What is the aim and final purpose of the Emperor Napoleon with this new departure?

His Majesty the King expresses the fear that the Emperor will push it as far as a breach with Prussia; and I cannot help feeling that this fear is justified, at least in the diplomatic sphere.

Confederation to Empire

I did not conceal from the ambassador that his communications would make this impression, and that at the present moment I should consider it wiser not to pursue it any further. But his instructions seem this time to be much more peremptory. M. Benedetti did declare, 'We shall not make war for that', but he forecast lasting ill-humour on the part of the Emperor and his government, which would have a fateful influence on the whole position.

From W.N. Medlicott and D.K. Coveney (eds.): *Bismarck and Europe* (1971)

K Bismarck considers war with France in conversation with a member of the Prussian Parliament in March 1867

Unhappily I believe in a war with France before long – her vanity, hurt by our victories, will drive her in that direction. Yet, since I do not know of any French or German interest requiring a resort to arms, I do not see it as certain. Only a country's most vital interests justify embarking on war – only its honour, which is not to be confused with so-called prestige. No statesman has a right to begin a war simply because, in his opinion, it is inevitable in a given period of time. If foreign ministers had followed their rulers and military commanders into the field History would record fewer wars. On the battlefield – and, what is far worse, in the hospitals – I have seen the flower of our youth struck down by wounds and disease ... You may rest assured that I shall never advise His Majesty to wage war unless the most vital interests of the Fatherland require it.

From Alan Palmer: *Bismarck* (1976)

L The Hohenzollern princes discuss accession to the Spanish throne, as recorded on 19 June 1870 in the diary of Major Max von Versen, Bismarck's agent in Madrid

The Hereditary Prince said that with a heavy heart but with the consciousness of acting in the interest of the State he asked the King's permission to accept. The letter was worded in such a way that the Hereditary Prince intimated that he was making a sacrifice for the renown of the family and the weal of the Fatherland; but it was at the same time phrased so that the King only needed to reply: 'no objection'. The Hereditary Prince repeated what he had said to me already several times, namely, that 'he had to say this because he was not acting either from self-interest or on any special impulse, and did not want to appear as a "climber" '. Bucher induced the younger brother King Frederick William IV of Prussia, Prince Karl Anton, to accompany this letter of the Hereditary Prince's with one of his own to the King in which he said: 'Only on grounds of Family Law did his son thus apply for permission and he trusted the King would have no objections to make.' The question now arose who was to go to the King. Bucher looked at me as if I should be the one. I said the best thing would be for Herr Bucher to go, for the King is furious that I am not at Posen. Then there came various scruples on Prince Karl Anton's part. What would France say about it? Would it not give rise to complications? I said: 'Bismarck says that is just what he is looking for.'

From W.N. Medlicott and D.K. Coveney (eds.): *Bismarck and Europe* (1971)

M The Ems Telegram 13 July 1870
(i) The dispatch from a Foreign Office official to Bismarck

His Majesty the King writes to me: 'Count Benedetti caught me on the Promenade and importunately requested me to authorise him to send a telegram at once saying I bound myself not to consent to the Hohenzollern candidature should they attempt to renew it at any future time; this I declined and rather sternly. One cannot enter *à tout jamais* into such an engagement. I, of course, told him that I had no news, but as he got his from Paris and Madrid sooner than I did, he must understand that my Government was taking no part in the matter.' Since then his Majesty has received a letter from Prince Karl Anton. His Majesty had informed Count Benedetti that he was expecting news from the Prince, but, having regard to the above unreasonable demand, his Majesty resolved, on the advice of Count Eulenburg and myself, not to receive Count Benedetti again, but merely to send him a message by an adjutant to the effect that his Majesty had now received from the Prince the confirmation of the news which Benedetti had already received from Paris, and that his Majesty had nothing further to say to the Ambassador. His Majesty leaves it to the decision of your Excellency whether this new demand of Benedetti and our refusal to comply therewith should not be forthwith communicated to our Ambassadors and to the press.

(ii) The version as edited and sent by Bismarck

After the news of the renunciation of the Prince of Hohenzollern had been officially communicated by the Spanish Government to the French Government, the French Ambassador in Ems nevertheless demanded that his Majesty should authorise him to telegraph to Paris, that his Majesty pledged himself for all future time never again to give his consent to the Hohenzollern resuming the candidature. His Majesty has thereupon declined to receive the Ambassador again and has informed him through the adjutant that he has nothing further to communicate to the Ambassador.

From W.N. Medlicott and D.K. Coveney (eds.): *Bismarck and Europe* (1971)

N The argument in Bavaria for entering the German Empire, as presented in the Upper House of the Bavarian Parliament by the Minister-President, Prince Hohenlohe

It seems to me that two facts, above all others, have tended to guide German policy into new paths, to modify the position of Bavaria, as it has developed during recent centuries, and to unite the country more closely to Germany. One of these facts is the awakened spirit of nationalism throughout the German people, and the other is the changed position of the German Great Powers.

When Bavaria became a kingdom in 1806 she reached the highest point of that policy which I have styled isolation, and which found its explanation, if not justification, in the general condition of the German Empire and the absence of any national feelings. Bavaria had, formally at least, attained full sovereignty. Yet a few years afterwards the kingdom surrendered important rights in favour of the German Confederation, and the deciding motive in this case was respect for the growing sense of nationality throughout the German people. When the war of liberation had begun, it was impossible to continue the policy of the Rhine Federation.

In the year 1866, after the dissolution of the German Federation, when Bavaria for the second time secured a doubtful freedom to determine her own course, the kingdom immediately hastened to sacrifice the independence she had secured in the convention of 22 August, apparently guided by the idea that German nationalism would make the pursuit of any other policy impossible except that which was expressed in the convention. You also, my lords, were witness of a similar turning point in Bavarian history in the autumn of 1867, when the acceptance or refusal of the convention therewith connected came before you for discussion. The majority of you at that time could not decide to secure that economic isolation of Bavaria which would necessarily have resulted in political isolation. After serious doubts, you made your determination and voted as you did, because a non-German policy was no longer possible in a German state. When in the summer of this year the decisive moment approached and it seemed possible for the last time to enter upon a course which would have replaced Bavaria in the position of 1806, you resisted the temptations which one party placed before the Bavarian people and which are rightly termed unpatriotic. You rejected that neutrality which would have led to an alliance with France. At that time a political opponent cried to me: 'Now the German Empire is complete.' The prophecy has been fulfilled, not, as a previous speaker has observed, because military alliance necessarily implies subordination to the power of the stronger ally; it has been fulfilled because German nationalism has become a power in this war and a force to which the preference for long-standing institutions must give way, and before which the antipathetic tendencies of the German races have disappeared.

From: *The Memoirs of Prince Chlodwig of Hohenlohe-Schillingsfürst* (1906)

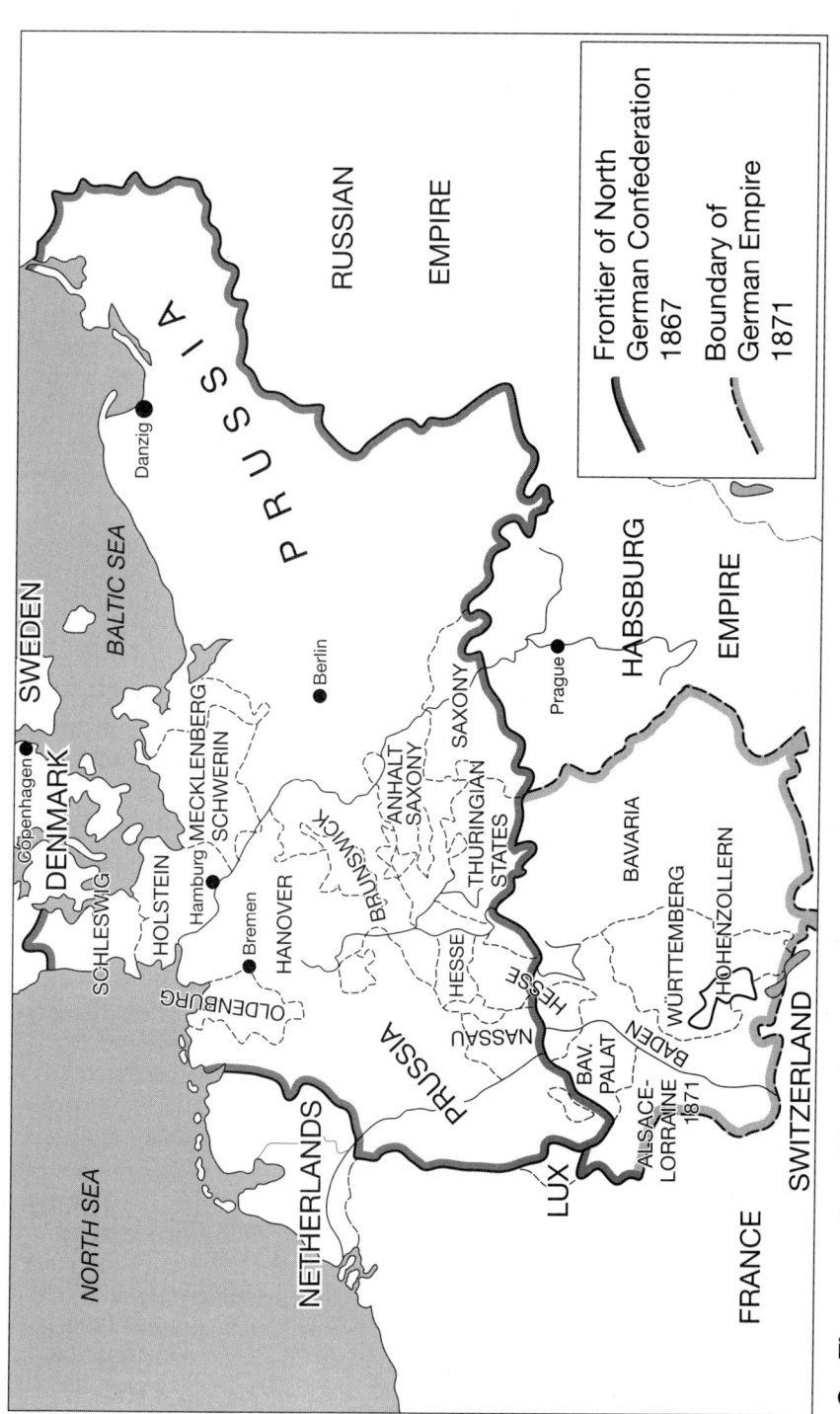

Bismarck and Prussian Domination in Germany 1862–71

O The expansion of Prussian power

Confederation to Empire

P A modern analyst explains why Prussia was victorious

The triumph of Prusso-Germany was, quite clearly, a triumph of its military systems: but ... behind the sweeping advances of the German columns and the controlled orchestrations of the general staff there lay a nation much better equipped and prepared for the conditions of modern warfare than any other in Europe. In 1870 the German states combined already possessed a larger population than France, and only disunity had disguised the fact: Germany had more miles of railway lines, better arranged for military purposes. Its gross national product and its iron and steel production were just then overtaking the French totals. Its coal production was two and a half times as great, and its consumption from modern energy was 50 per cent larger ... The army's short-service system was offensive to liberals inside and outside the country but it mobilised the manpower of the nation for warlike purposes more effectively than the *laissez-faire* west or the backward agrarian east.

From Paul Kennedy: *The Rise and Fall of the Great Powers* (1988)

Questions

1. How do Sources A and B help us to understand Bismarck's view of the role of the Prussian monarchy? **(6 marks)**
2. How far does Source C explain why William I's non-attendance at Frankfurt frustrated Austria's plans? **(4 marks)**
3. Using Source D and your own knowledge, explain how Bismarck improved Russo-Prussian relations in 1863. **(4 marks)**
4. Using your knowledge of the causes of the Prusso-Austrian war, explain why Bismarck states in Source E that 'much more depends on the attitude of the non-German Great Powers'. **(7 marks)**
5. In what ways can Sources F and G both be identified as steps on the way to the Austro-Prussian war of 1866? **(8 marks)**
6. Using your own knowledge and Source H, account for Bismarck's anxiety to restrain William I and the Prussian generals after Königgrätz. **(6 marks)**
7. How far do Sources I, J, K, L and M suggest that Bismarck was responsible for provoking war between France and the German states in 1870? **(10 marks)**
8. With reference to Source N, explain why the South German states entered the German Empire in 1871. **(6 marks)**
9. How much does the map in Source O complement Source P in explaining why Prussian power increased so much between 1862 and 1871? **(7 marks)**

5 BISMARCK'S INTERNAL POLICIES 1871–90

After the creation of the German Empire in 1871 the constitution of the North German Confederation was simply extended to cover the whole territory. Thus the government of the new state was in the hands of the Emperor and the Imperial Chancellor, Bismarck, assisted by the 58 members of the Federal Council (*Bundesrat*), representing the 25 state governments [A, B]. In addition, the Emperor together with the *Bundesrat* and the *Reichstag* exercised legislative power. In 1871 the *Reichstag* consisted of 397 members, elected by universal adult male suffrage, serving for a five year term and possessing the power to accept or reject legislation [C].

There was no chance that any of the political parties in the *Reichstag*, whatever their numbers or whether they were liberal, conservative, socialist or Catholic, could form the government. The *Reichstag* could not appoint or dismiss the Chancellor who was omnipotent while he enjoyed the support of the Emperor. Initially Bismarck also had the support of the majority of conservatives and the National Liberals, the largest party in the *Reichstag*, and this collaboration produced a number of liberal measures [D].

The French war indemnity paid under the terms of the peace treaty, together with railway construction, produced a post-war boom leading to stock market speculation [E], followed by a collapse in share prices in 1873. To some extent this undermined the popularity of the National Liberals who argued for a free market economy and, since newspapers like the conservative *Kreuzzeitung* identified Jews with the stock market, it also contributed to a revival of anti-Semitism for the first time since the 1820s [F, G].

In 1871 Bismarck, judging that Catholics gave their first loyalty to the Pope rather than the state, introduced the first anti-Catholic legislation in Prussia, which marked the beginning of discriminatory laws and culminated in those of May 1873 known as the *Kulturkampf* ('struggle between cultures'). As a result, many of the Catholic hierarchy defied the state. The archbishops of Cologne and of Posen, together with two other bishops, were imprisoned while 1300 parishes were deprived of their priests [H–J]. Bismarck stated that the reasons for the *Kulturkampf* were political rather than religious. He was provoked by the creation of a strong, essentially Catholic bloc, the Centre Party, led by Ludwig Windthorst. As a policy the *Kulturkampf* failed. Under persecution the Catholics became more united and in the January 1874 election the Centre Party increased its strength from 63 to 91 seats [K].

Confederation to Empire

By 1875 Bismarck's priorities were changing. He was concerned by the growth of the Socialist Party and introduced his first anti-socialist bill in the *Reichstag* in 1876, only to see it defeated through opposition by his former allies the National Liberals. In the same period, thanks to the existing economic depression, there was increasing pressure to introduce tariffs to protect both agriculture and industry [L]. Bismarck was prepared to respond but, as had happened to his proposed anti-socialist laws, the introduction of tariffs was opposed by the National Liberals. He allowed the anti-Catholic laws to lapse in the hope of conciliating the Centre Party. Then he exploited two attempts to assassinate William I in 1878. These he blamed on the Socialists in order to justify the dissolution of the *Reichstag* and the calling of a snap election. The National Liberals and Social Democrats both lost seats. Bismarck was now able to pass an Anti-Socialist Act [M, N]. This was followed by the introduction of tariffs in 1879 [O].

As his anti-Catholic legislation failed to undermine the Catholic hierarchy so also Bismarck's anti-socialist laws failed to weaken the Social Democratic Party which continued to grow in numbers [P, Q]. However, Bismarck attempted to woo the German workers away from socialism by more positive means. A social welfare policy was introduced in the 1880s, establishing accident insurance in 1881, health insurance in 1883 and old age pensions in 1889 [R].

But in the 1880s Bismarck experienced increasing problems with the *Reichstag* and used whatever means he could to ensure its compliance. Two Peace Bills were passed in 1885 and 1887, marking the virtual end of the *Kulturkampf* and thus creating the possibility of more support from the Centre Party. Also in 1887 he fought a *Reichstag* election in an atmosphere of artificial crisis, using the supposed threat to Germany posed by General Boulanger, the revanchist French Minister for War. In this way he was successful in gaining a majority to support his policies. Bismarck was also worried by the prospect of the accession of Frederick III to the throne [S]. However, when Frederick did succeed his father, William I, in 1888 he survived only three months before dying of cancer.

Unfortunately for Bismarck there were real problems with the new Kaiser, William II. After a good start, relations between the two men soon deteriorated [T]. William was critical of Bismarck's attitude to the socialists and the two men disagreed over a solution to the 1889 miners' strike. There was increasing frustration on both sides and when Bismarck surprisingly submitted his resignation in March 1890 William II equally surprisingly accepted it [U, V].

A   Power in Imperial Germany as seen by a modern observer

The Empire did not emanate from the will of the people. Sovereignty resided in 22 rulers – four kings, six grand dukes, four dukes and eight

Bismarck's Internal Policies 1871–90

princes – who, in company with the senates of three free cities, created the Empire by a voluntary act of association. In theory these rulers were all equal; in practice no one denied that the Prussian ruler was more equal than the remainder; as German Emperor he was head of the imperial executive and civil service and supreme war-lord of all the armed forces of the Empire.

From William Carr: *A History of Germany 1815–1990* (1991)

B An English view of the new German Empire – *The Times*, 20 January 1871
In 1871 Germany starts independent, ardently patriotic, almost purely national ... The Parliament in which Germany will be represented has not yet been constituted, but if there be anything safe in political prediction it is that this Parliament will reflect the instincts and impulses which have welded the nation into one. There will be an inevitable tendency in the Federal Legislature and Administration to break down the independent authorities which the Minor States have reserved for themselves or have been suffered by Prussia to retain.

From M. Gorman: *The Unification of Germany* (1989)

C Bismarck writing of the value of adult male suffrage in relation to the parliament of the North German Confederation
At the moment of decision the masses will stand on the side of kingship regardless of whether the latter happens to follow a liberal or a conservative tendency ... May I indeed express it as a conviction based on long experience that the artificial system of indirect and class elections is much more dangerous than that of direct and general suffrage, because it prevents contact between the highest authority and the healthy elements that constitute the core and the mass of the people. In a country with monarchical traditions and loyal sentiments the general suffrage, by eliminating the influence of the liberal bourgeois classes will also lead to monarchical elections.

From Gordon Craig: *Germany 1866–1945* (1978)

D A contemporary English view of Bismarck's power – Lady Emily Russell, the wife of the British Ambassador, writing in 1880
The initiated know that the emperor ... has allowed Prince Bismarck to have his own way in everything; and the great chancellor revels in the absolute power he has acquired and does as he pleases. He lives in the country and governs the German Empire without even taking the trouble to consult the emperor about his plans, who only learns what is being done from the documents to which his signature is necessary,

and which His Majesty signs without questions or hesitation. Never has a subject been granted so much irresponsible power from his sovereign, and never has a minister inspired a nation with more abject individual, as well as general, terror before. No wonder, then, that the crown prince should be worried at a state of things which he has not more personal power or influence to remedy than anyone else in Prussia, whilst Prince Bismarck lives and terrorises over Germany from Friedrichsruh with the emperor's tacit and cheerful consent.

Bismarck has gradually appointed a ministry of clerks out of the government offices, who do as they are told by him, and he has so terrified the *Bundesrat*, by threatening to resign whenever they disagreed with him, that they now vote entirely in obedience to his instructions. He now expects that at the next general election he will, by careful management, obtain the absolute majority he requires to carry through his new taxation and commercial policy.

If Bismarck should ever die suddenly from indigestion, which his doctors fear and predict, the difficulty of reforming the general abuses which his personal administration has created will be great, and will impose a hard and ungrateful task on the sovereign, who will have to find and appoint the ministers capable of re-establishing constitutionalism in Prussia.

From G.E. Buckle (ed.): *The Letters of Queen Victoria* (1926–30)

E   Financial speculation in Berlin 1871–73, as described in his memoirs by a Berliner, Felix Philippi

Everyone, everyone flew into the flame: the shrewd capitalist and the inexperienced petty bourgeois, the general and the waiter, the woman of the world, the poor piano teacher and the market woman; people speculated in porter's lodges and theatre cloakrooms, in the studio of the artist and the quiet home of the scholar; the *Droschke* [cab] driver on his bench and Aujuste in the kitchen followed the rapid rise of the market with expertise and feverish interest. The market had bullish orgies; millions, coined out of the ground, were won; national prosperity rose to apparently unimagined heights. A shower of gold rained down on the drunken city.

From Gordon Craig: *Germany 1866–1945* (1978)

F   Theodore Fontane, a German novelist, writing to a friend in November 1880 foreshadows the revival of anti-Semitism in Imperial Germany

I have been philosemitic since my childhood and have never experienced anything but kindness from Jews. Nevertheless I have a feeling of their guilt, their unlimited arrogance, to such an extent, that I

Bismarck's Internal Policies 1871–90

not only wish them a serious defeat, but desire it. And of this I am convinced, if they do not suffer it now and do not change now, a terrible visitation will come upon them, albeit in times that we will not live to see.

From Gerhard Masur: *Imperial Berlin* (1970)

G Evidence of the revival of anti-Semitism from *Kreuzzeitung*, a conservative newspaper, in June 1875

The financial and economic policy of the newly founded German Empire gives many observers the impression of being purely the policy of the banker. It is no wonder, for Herr von Bleichröder [Bismarck's own banker] is himself a banker ... and Herr Camphausen, the Prussian Finance Minister, is the brother of a banker. If on the other hand, the fiscal and economic policy of the German Empire gives one the impression of a Jewish policy, that too is explicable since Herr von Bleichröder is himself a Jew ... Messrs Lasker, Bamberger and H.B. Oppenheimer, who are also Jews, are the actual leaders of the so-called National Liberal majority in the *Reichstag* and in the Prussian parliament. Jewish banking houses influence the nomination of ministers, and try to make the states and statesmen dependent upon them.

From Gordon Craig: *Germany 1866–1945* (1978)

H Bismarck on the *Kulturkampf* in March 1873

The question that confronts us becomes in my opinion distorted and the light in which we regard it falsified, if it is looked on as a confessional or religious one. It is essentially political. It is not a matter of an attack by a Protestant dynasty upon the Catholic Church, as our Catholic fellow citizens are being told, it is not a matter of a struggle between faith and unbelief. What we have here is the age-old struggle for power, as old as the human race itself, between kingship and the priestly caste, a struggle for power that goes far beyond the coming of our Saviour to this World ... the struggle for power that filled German history from the Middle Ages until the destruction of the German Empire.

From Gordon Craig: *Germany 1866–1945* (1978)

I Bismarck's precise instructions to the Prussian Minister of Public Worship, 1872

What precisely do you want me to do? (Adalbert Falk, Prussian Minister of Public Worship, to Bismarck)
To restore the rights of the state over the church and do it with the least possible fuss. (Bismarck to Falk)

From Alan Palmer: *Bismarck* (1976)

Confederation to Empire

J The British reaction to the *Kulturkampf*, expressed in a private letter by Odo Russell, the British Ambassador, in October 1872

I fancy that Bismarck utterly underrates the power of the Church. Thinking himself more infallible than the Pope he cannot tolerate two infallibles in Europe . . . Hitherto the anti-clerical measures have produced the very thing the Vatican was working for through the Oecumenical Council, namely unity and discipline in the clergy under an infallible head, or the Prussian military system applied to the Church.

From Alan Palmer: *Bismarck* (1976)

K A Protestant theologian comments in 1880 on the effects of the *Kulturkampf*

It is a bad thing when the state punishes actions that are considered purely religious ones and as a matter of conscience, and, when in consequence, the punishment loses that character of punishment in the eyes of the people and becomes its opposite. It hardly promotes the authority of the state and its sanctions when in the eyes of many of the better class even imprisonment begins to be regarded as a title of greater respect. In short, the state cannot conduct a war against a large part of its own population without causing, on all sides, a profound injury to the moral consciousness.

From Gordon Craig: *Germany 1866–1945* (1978)

L In a declaration in March 1877, 400 representatives of industry and agriculture from Westphalia indicate their support for the introduction of tariffs

  I   In view of the impending renewal of commercial treaties and tariffs, the depression which has lasted for many years necessitates that agriculture and industry proceed in the future with the same solidarity which exists in reality without prejudicing individual political ties.
  II For the promotion of general economic interests it is necessary:
   (a) to preserve and to develop home production as the first condition of general welfare;
   (b) the main factors for the attainment of this aim are low freight rates, well considered commercial treaties and tariffs, and a rational system of taxation, all based on actual conditions;
   (c) the discovery of the actual needs is to be reached through the questioning and consultation of experts;
   (d) the reform of the land and building tax and the mining tax which are to be covered through indirect taxation;

(e) excepting the removal of direct and indirect export premiums enjoyed by foreign agricultural products, but which we spurn, German agriculture wants no further favours.

From I.N. Lambi: *Free Trade & Protection in Germany 1868–1879* (1963)

M The wide scope of the Anti-Socialist Law – part of the text of the Law passed by the *Reichstag* in 1878

1 Societies which aim at the overthrow of the existing political or social order through social democratic, socialistic, or communistic endeavours are to be prohibited

This applies also to societies in which social democratic, socialistic, or communistic endeavours aiming at the overthrow of the existing political or social order are manifested in a manner dangerous to the public peace, and particularly to the harmony among the classes of the population.

Associations of every kind are the same as societies ...

4 The [police] is empowered:
- (1) To attend all sessions and meetings of the society.
- (2) To call and conduct membership assemblies.
- (3) To inspect the books, papers and cash assets, as well as to demand information about the affairs of the society.
- (4) To forbid the carrying out of resolutions which are apt to further the endeavours described in **1**, para. 2.
- (5) To transfer to qualified persons the duties of the officers or other leading organs of the society.
- (6) To take charge of and manage the funds ...

28 For districts or localities where the public safety is menaced by the endeavours described in **1**, para. 2, the following regulations may be decreed, in case they are not already permitted by state law, with the consent of the *Bundesrat* for a period not exceeding one year:
- (1) that meetings may take place only after the consent of the police authority has been obtained; this limitation does not extend to meetings called for the purposes of an announced election to the *Reichstag* or to the diets of the states;
- (2) that the distribution of publications shall not take place on public roads, streets, squares or other public places;
- (3) that the residence in districts or localities of persons from whom danger to public safety and order is to be feared may be forbidden;
- (4) that the possession, bearing, importation, and sale of weapons is to be forbidden, limited, or made conditional upon certain requirements.

Confederation to Empire

> The *Reichstag* must be informed immediately, that is, upon its first reassembling, about any decree that has been issued under the foregoing provisions.
>
> The decrees are to be announced in the *Reichsanzieger* [the official state gazette] and by whatever manner is prescribed for local police orders.
>
> Whoever, knowingly or after public notice is given, acts in contravention of these regulations, or of the decisions based thereon, is to be punished by fine not exceeding one thousand marks, or with arrest or imprisonment not exceeding six months.

From V.L. Lidtke: *The Outlawed Party – Social Democracy in Germany 1878–1890* (1966)

N Support for Bismarck's anti-socialist legislation comes from the Court Chaplain (Albert Stöcker) in Berlin in 1880

With respect to Social Democracy two different kinds of erroneous conceptions are prevalent. One group of economists sees Social Democracy as something quite harmless, as a system of social reforms aimed at achieving the welfare of one's neighbours. They forget the immoral tendencies connected with it and the war against Christianity that is bound up with it, and – attracted by the intellectual energy of the Social Democratic Party, by its dedication, and by its willingness to make sacrifices – they have almost nothing but good things to say of the movement. This conception is certainly wrong – Social Democracy is not just a movement for social reforms; as it portrays itself in Germany and as it has portrayed itself for decades in pamphlets, books and assemblies it is a new conception of the world – a conception which, once it has taken hold of people, prises them away from Christianity, patriotism and German morality.

From W.M. Simon: *Germany in the Age of Bismarck* (1968)

O Bismarck justifies the introduction of tariffs in a speech in the *Reichstag* in May 1879

The only country (which persists in a policy of free trade) is England, and that will not last long. France and America have departed completely from this line; Austria instead of lowering her tariffs has made them higher; Russia has done the same ... Therefore to be alone the dupe of an honourable conviction cannot be expected from Germany for ever. By opening wide the doors of our state to the imports of foreign countries, we have become the dumping ground for the production of those countries ... Since we have become swamped by the surplus production of foreign nations, our prices have been

Bismarck's Internal Policies 1871-90

depressed; and the development of our industries and our entire economic position has suffered in consequence.

Let us finally close our doors and erect some barriers, as we have proposed to you, in order to reserve for German industries at least the home market, which because of German good nature, has been exploited by foreigners. The problem of a large export trade is always a very delicate one; there are no new lands to discover, the world has been circumnavigated, and we can no longer find abroad new purchasers of importance to whom we can send our goods...

I see that those countries which have adopted protection are prospering, and that those countries which have free trade are deteriorating.

From Andrina Stiles: *The Unification of Germany 1815-1890* (1990)

P   A modern historian assesses the impact of Bismarck's anti-socialist actions

Bismarck's use of the state of siege opened the eyes of many of those who had hoped to reach an accommodation with the government by making concessions and made them aware that the Chancellor was not engaged in a policy of petty harassment but was bent on the complete destruction of the party organisation and the personal ruin of its members. Many Socialists admitted later that it was the spectacle of policemen uprooting people from homes in which they had lived for thirty years, destroying their livelihoods, and sending them on the road to beg that convinced them that they must fight back.

From Gordon Craig: *Germany 1866-1945* (1978)

Q   The failure of Bismarck's anti-socialist policy, evidenced by a report from Berlin's Chief of Police, 1889

The antagonism between the classes has sharpened and a gulf separates the workers from the rest of society. The expectation of victory has grown. The German socialist party holds first rank in Europe because of its superior organisation. It has outstanding leaders, especially Bebel and Liebknecht, and it is united. Clandestine newspapers continue to appear in spite of all confiscatory measures. The trades union movement increases steadily, and the party can look forward to considerable gains in the next elections to the *Reichstag*.

From Gerhard Masur: *Imperial Berlin* (1970)

R   Bismarck justifies his social welfare programme in a speech in the *Reichstag* on 2 April 1881

Deputy Richter [leader of the Progressive Party] has called attention to the state's responsibility for what it does in the field which it is entering today. Well, gentlemen, I think that the state can also be held responsible for what it omits to do. I think that those who repudiate the intervention of the state . . . for the protection of the weaker expose themselves for their part to the suspicion that they wish to exploit the resources of which they dispose, whether these be capitalistic or rhetorical or other, for the purposes of gaining a following, of oppressing others, of laying the foundations for a party domination, and that they become annoyed as soon as they are disturbed in this enterprise by any government action . . . In my opinion the principle of compulsory insurance entails the state taking over the enterprise.

From W.M. Simon: *Germany in the Age of Bismarck* (1968)

S Bismarck's attitude to William II (from a letter by Holstein, a senior Foreign Office official, in October 1888)

He follows the triumphal march of the young Kaiser from afar with feelings of a soured old coquette.

From Alan Palmer: *Bismarck* (1976)

T The fall of Bismarck, as described by Theodore Fontane, writing in May 1890

Bismarck had no greater admirer than I; my wife never read me one of his speeches or letters or sayings without my feeling a real enchantment. The world has seldom seen a greater genius, seldom a greater humorist. But one thing he always lacked: nobility. Its opposite, which finally took the hateful form of petty spite, ran through his life, and because of this lack of nobility he finally came to ruin, and in this lack of nobility is to be found the explanation of the relative indifference with which even his admirers watched him forced to leave . . . It is fortunate we are rid of him, and many, many questions will now be handled better, more honourably, more clearly than before.

From Gordon Craig: *Germany 1866–1945* (1978)

Bismarck's Internal Policies 1871–90

U 'Dropping the Pilot' – a cartoon in *Punch*, 29 March 1890

V   Bismarck's legacy – the view of Max Weber, a German sociologist, in 1917
Bismarck left behind him as a political heritage a nation without any political education, far below the level which, in this respect, it had reached 20 years earlier. Above all, he left behind a nation without any political will, accustomed to allow the great statesman at its head to look after its policy for it. Moreover, as a consequence of his misuse of the monarchy as a cover for his own interests in the struggle of political parties, he left a nation accustomed to submit, under the label of constitutional monarchy, to anything which was decided for it, without criticising the political qualifications of those who now occupied Bismarck's empty place and who with incredible ingenuousness now took the reins of power into their hands.

From William Carr: *A History of Germany 1815–1990* (1991)

Questions

1. According to the evidence in Sources A, B and D, what was the basis of Bismarck's power in the German Empire? **(5 marks)**
2. In Source C, what evidence is there of the effects of universal male suffrage in Germany between 1871 and 1890? **(5 marks)**
3. How far do Sources E, F and G explain the revival of anti-Semitism in Imperial Germany? **(7 marks)**
4. Using Sources H, I, J and K, and your own knowledge, examine Bismarck's reasons for introducing the *Kulturkampf* and explain why he failed to achieve his objectives. **(10 marks)**
5. Using Sources L and O and your own knowledge, explain why Bismarck introduced tariffs in 1879. **(8 marks)**
6. 'Bismarck's anti-socialist policies had no chance of being successful.' How far do Sources M, N, P and Q justify this statement? **(10 marks)**
7. In Source R, what motives are identified as underlying Bismarck's social welfare programme? **(4 marks)**
8. Which of the Sources shows the more realistic understanding of the 'Fall of Bismarck', S or T? **(8 marks)**
9. Using your own knowledge of the history of Germany between 1890 and 1914, comment on the accuracy of the views expressed in Source V. **(10 marks)**

6 BISMARCK'S FOREIGN POLICY 1871–90

By 1871 Bismarck had achieved the immediate objectives of his policy. A German Empire, dominated by Prussia, had been created from the non-Austrian territories of the German Confederation. From this date onwards his aim was the defence and consolidation of this German Empire. However, between 1871 and his fall from power in 1890 Bismarck apparently experienced an almost permanent sense of crisis.

This was in part the result of a fear of being attacked. The German Empire had no easily defendable frontiers and was bordered by three of the major European powers. Of these, France was a sworn enemy while the Austrian Empire might well look for an opportunity to avenge its defeat in 1866. For Bismarck these dangers were increased by the number of Catholics within the German Empire (see Chapter 5). For these reasons isolation of France was a major aim of Bismarck's policy after 1871 and this was achieved by the signing of the *Dreikaiserbund* (Three Emperors' League) in October 1873, which had the additional benefit of cementing good relations with Austria [A–D].

However, the 1875 'War Scare' showed that Bismarck's position was not necessarily secure. Bismarck's determination to threaten France was stimulated not only by French backing for Alsatian Catholics during the *Kulturkampf*, but also by the speed with which France had paid off her war indemnity and by French rearmament. The crisis was precipitated by an anti-French campaign in the German press, almost certainly inspired by Bismarck [E]. This produced fear in France and among the other European powers [F, G] of a new German attack on the Third Republic. Britain and Italy both sent cautious messages to Berlin urging peace, and these were reinforced when the Russian foreign minister Gortschakov asked Bismarck for specific assurances of his peaceful intentions. This infuriated the German Chancellor who had only intended to warn France not to risk another war.

From 1875 onwards Bismarck could not ignore the developing events in the Balkans. Throughout the period 1875–8 his main objective was to preserve the *Dreikaiserbund* and thus the isolation of France. At the same time he was determined that the German Empire should not become directly involved in the Balkan crises [H].

In 1878, following its defeat by Russia, Turkey was forced to sign the Peace Treaty of San Stefano, which the other major European powers considered totally unsatisfactory. Bismarck as 'honest broker' in the dispute acted as chairman of the Berlin Congress (13 June – 13 July 1878) which sought to modify the Treaty. The result was temporary peace in the Balkans and the preservation of the *Dreikaiserbund*. However, Bismarck had failed to achieve genuine Austro-Russian reconciliation and neither power believed it had received sufficient German support [I, J].

After the Congress, Russo-German relations continued to deteriorate. The 1879 German tariff law which discriminated against Russian grain imports worsened the situation. Bismarck approached Britain with the possibility of an alliance, but this produced no result. Against the wishes of William I, he then worked to secure an alliance with Austria. By threatening to resign, he persuaded the German Emperor to sign the Dual Alliance, a secret treaty with Austria in October 1879. Even this did not fulfil all Bismarck's hopes since it did not secure the promise of Austrian military assistance in the event of a war with France [K-M].

Fortunately, Russo-German relations showed signs of improvement and Alexander II sent Saburov to Berlin to continue this process. Subsequently Bismarck exerted pressure on Austria to act with restraint regarding Russia, while at the same time assuring the Russians that the Dual Alliance did not commit Germany to defend Austria in the event of a Russian attack. Thus he was able to secure a renewal of the *Dreikaiserbund* in June 1881 [N–P].

There were increased fears of tension in the Balkans stimulated by increased pan-Slav influence on Tsar Alexander III. This was one of the reasons why Bismarck favoured the Triple Alliance, signed with Austria and Italy in May 1882, which gave increased security to Austria [Q]. At the same time he worked for good relations with the Tsar and was able to secure a renewal of the *Dreikaiserbund* in 1884. He then persuaded German financiers to subscribe to Russian loans floated on the Berlin stock market.

By the late 1870s a peaceful bourgeois republic had emerged in France and Bismarck was happy to encourage French colonial ambitions to turn attention away from Alsace-Lorraine. The desire to improve Franco-German relations was certainly one of the reasons why Bismarck backed German colonial growth in the years 1884–5. These relations reached a high point at the 1884–5 Berlin Conference on Central Africa. Commercial motives and the internal political situation also provided reasons for Bismarck's colonial policy [R–T]. The election of the anti-German Freycinet government in France, with General Boulanger as Minister of War, in 1886 ended Franco-German cooperation. In the same period Russia's attempts to increase her influence in Bulgaria damaged Austro-Russian relations. Bismarck feared that Russian attempts to raise money in France would lead to close Franco-Russian relations [U].

In 1887 Tsar Alexander III refused to renew the *Dreikaiserbund*. However, he agreed to separate negotiations with Germany and these led to the signing of the Reinsurance Treaty in June 1887 [V]. This, for the

Bismarck's Foreign Policy 1871–90

time being, lessened the danger of a Franco-Russian *rapprochement* but committed Germany to supporting Russian ambitions in Bulgaria against the perceived interests of Austria. In spite of the new treaty, Bismarck still acted to restrain Russia's Balkan ambitions by effectively vetoing a new Russian attempt to raise a loan in Germany in November 1887.

From 1871 the principal objective of Bismarck's foreign policy was to prevent the convergence of two potential conflicts – the Franco-German and the Austro-Russian. While he remained in power he very largely achieved his aim [W].

A Bismarck shows his wariness towards France, in a dispatch dated February 1874

I am convinced that the danger which threatens us from France starts from the moment when France appears to the courts of Europe to be capable of making an alliance again, which it was not under Thiers, and is not yet under MacMahon ... MacMahon is perhaps not a politician in the sense that Count Andrassy uses the word; but he is ultramontane, almost as strongly as his wife, and can control this leaning and his hatred of us so little that he has not been able to bring himself, since peace was concluded, to exchange even the most common courtesies with Fieldmarshal Manteuffel ...

From W.N. Medlicott and D.K. Coveney (eds.): *Bismarck and Europe* (1971)

B A first step towards French isolation – the text of the German-Russian Military Convention, 6 May 1873

His Majesty the Emperor of Germany and His Majesty the Emperor of all the Russias, wishing to give practical form to the thought that governs their close accord, that is to say, of consolidating the present state of peace in Europe and eliminating the chances of war that could disturb it, have authorised their Fieldmarshals Count Moltke and Count Berg to conclude the following military convention:
1 If one of the two empires is attacked by a European power, it will be supported with the least possible delay by an army of 200 000 effective troops.
2 This military convention is concluded in a spirit which is devoid of hostility towards any nation or any government.
3 If one of the two contracting parties wishes to denounce the present military convention, it shall be obliged to do so two years before it can be considered as annulled.

From W.N. Medlicott and D.K. Coveney (eds.): *Bismarck and Europe* (1971)

C The terms of the *Dreikaiserbund*, 1873

His Majesty the Emperor of Austria and King of Hungary and His Majesty the Emperor of all the Russias wishing to give a practical form

to the thought governing their close entente.
With the aim of consolidating the peace which exists at the moment in Europe, and having their heart set on eliminating the chances of war which could disturb it.
Convinced that this aim could not be better attained than by a direct personal agreement between the rulers, an agreement independent of any changes which might occur in their administrations, have agreed upon the following points:

1. Their Majesties promise mutually, even though the interests of their country might differ with respect to particular questions, to consult together so that these divergencies do not take precedence over considerations of a higher order which may be preoccupying them. Their Majesties have decided to oppose any move to separate them with regard to principles which they consider themselves alone capable of assuring, and, if necessary, to impose the maintenance of peace in Europe against all attempts to destroy it, from whatever quarter they come.
2. In the case of an attack coming from a third power threatening to compromise the peace of Europe Their Majesties are mutually bound to come to an agreement first amongst themselves, without seeking or contracting new alliances, in order to agree on the line of conduct that they will follow in common.
3. If, in following this agreement, military action became necessary, it would be regulated by a special convention to be concluded between their Majesties.
4. If one of the high contracting parties, wishing to regain independence of action, desired to denounce the present agreement, it would be required to give two years' notice so as to give the other party time to make suitable alternative arrangements.

(Schönbrunn, 25 May/6 June 1873   Francois Joseph   Alexandre)

His Majesty the Emperor of Germany, having taken note of the above agreement, drawn up and signed at Schönbrunn by Their Majesties the Emperor of Austria and King of Hungary and the Emperor of all the Russias, and finding the content conformable to the thought governing the agreement signed at St Petersburg between Their Majesties the Emperor William and the Emperor Alexander, accedes to all the stipulations therein.

Their Majesties the Emperor and King William and the Emperor and King Francis Joseph, approving and signing this act of accession, will bring it to the notice of His Majesty the Emperor Alexander.

(Schönbrunn, 22 October 1873   Guillaume   Francois Joseph)

From W.N. Medlicott and D.K. Coveney (eds.): *Bismarck and Europe* (1971)

Bismarck's Foreign Policy 1871–90

D Bismarck attacks the German Roman Catholic priests in a speech in the *Reichstag*, 10 February 1872

The government cannot avoid the remarkable observation that the Roman Catholic clergy is national in all other lands. Only Germany makes an exception. The Polish clergy adhere to the Polish national movement, the Italian to the Italian ... Only in Germany is there the peculiar phenomenon that the *clergy* has a more *international* character ... The Catholic Church, even when she obstructs the development of Germany for the sake of foreign nations, is closer to its heart than the development of the German Empire ... [Windthorst: 'Proof!'] I cannot find an insult in that. [Call from the *Zentrum* and Right: 'Proof!'] *Ach*, gentlemen, search your own hearts. [Long, lasting laughter.]

From D.G. Williamson: *Bismarck and Germany 1862–1890* (1986)

E Bismarck's fears of France, as conveyed to Lord Derby by the British Ambassador on 27 April 1875

My Austrian colleague, Count Karolyi, called today and confided to me the substance of a conversation he had yesterday with Prince Bismarck at the FO as follows: The Prince, he said, began by telling that he was not – 'on his honour' – responsible for the articles in the press, especially the *Post*, which spoke with suspicion of the intentions and sympathies of Austria. He looked upon Austria as Germany's best friend and ally, but what the papers said about French armaments was true – the creation of the fourth battalion would give France 270 more battalions than before the late war, and a so-called peace establishment which could only be intended to enable the French army to take the field at any moment without calling in the reserves.

Prince Bismarck went on to explain in detail the various reasons which convinced him that France intended to attack Germany but he admitted that the military authorities did not expect the French army would be ready for war before the year 1877.

If the French, Prince Bismarck said, continued their preparations on the present scale, and that their intentions of attacking Germany admitted of no further doubt, it would be manifestly the duty of the German Government to take the initiative so as to put a stop to war by energetic measures.

From W.N. Medlicott and D.K. Coveney (eds.): *Bismarck and Europe* (1971)

F Bismarck and the German press – part of a despatch (from Gontaut-Biron to Decazes, the French Foreign Minister, 21 April 1875

This evening I dined with the English Ambassador, and after dinner I took the opportunity to have a chat with M. de Radowitz. [Gontaut-Biron spoke of the concern aroused recently by rumours of war.] Radowitz blamed untimely or over-zealous attacks by the press, but he was sure that it would be a mistake to think of any newspapers. 'The *Nationalzeitung* amongst others,' he said, 'is too important a paper to be influenced in the way you imagine, and it is not the only one in this position. If we tried to put pressure on it and it disagreed, the matter could be the subject of a question in the Chamber and even of lively debates. And is this pressure by the government as easy as you think?' – (and it is to this that I wish especially to draw Your Excellency's attention) – 'What will they keep repeating to us in the name of the parties which constitute the majority? You are reassured as to the present: perhaps! but can you answer for the future? Can you give your assurance that France, regaining its former prosperity, and having reorganised its military forces, will not then find alliances which it lacks at the moment, and that then these resentments that she cannot fail to foster, and that she naturally feels at the loss of these two provinces, will not drive her inexorably to declare war on Germany? . . . and if we have allowed France to revive, to expand, have we not everything to fear? . . . But if France's inmost thoughts are bent on revenge – and it cannot be otherwise – why wait to attack her until she has gathered her forces and contracted alliances? Agree, in fact, that politically, philosophically, and *even from a Christian point of view*, these deductions are well-founded and such fears are bound to guide Germany.'

The Austrian Ambassador very recently indicated to me this way of looking to our interests, but never has the Chancellor's attitude been revealed to me so clearly, so neatly, or with such authority . . .

From W.N. Medlicott and D.K. Coveney (eds.): *Bismarck and Europe* (1971)

G German fear of international complications, expressed in a dispatch from Bülow, the Foreign Secretary, on 3 June 1875

We now have a decided impression that strong anxiety regarding our policy has taken firm hold in England, and has spread from there on to the Continent. We believe it is genuine and not put on for other purposes. The only question is whence it arose. The fears did not originate in England, but have flowed into it and have found there a soil evidently suitable for their growth. The most obvious source lies in the much spoken of correspondence in *The Times* dated from Paris, on May 6th. We now know that it was really written there, but that its great influence was due to its appearing in that world-wide newspaper.

The British Government has not confined itself, as did Lord Derby in the extract from his speech of May 31st, which was telegraphed to us, to the task of calming the mutual trepidations of Germany and France with as little ostentation as possible. But we have learned, and naturally with regret, from St Petersburg and Vienna, that the British Government has been pursuing its misconceived attempt at soothing even there. We have it on the very best authority that in both capitals British influence has officially brought a charge against us of threatening to endanger peace and of desiring war in the first instance, if you please, against Austria. This is the insinuation made to the Austrian Cabinet by the British Embassy according to this communication . . .

From E.T.S. Dugdale (ed.): *German Diplomatic Documents, 1871–1914* (1930)

H Bismarck makes clear in a speech to the *Reichstag* on 5 December 1876 that he does not intend direct German involvement in the Balkans
So in the Eastern question we have set ourselves a task; and if I characterise it the questioner will gather that the customs question has no place in this programme, and that he must separate the two things: policy by itself and the customs question by itself. In Turkey we have the interests, which I have already explained, of general sympathy with our fellow Christians, and if the previous speaker quoted a report that he himself treats as apocryphal, that I am supposed to have said that in the whole of the Orient there is no interest that is worth the revenues of a single Pomeranian manor, that is wrong. In all such legends there is a grain of truth, and always a bit of falsehood too. [Much laughter] What I said was: I will not advise participation of Germany in these things as long as I see no interest for Germany in it which – forgive the blunt expression – would be worth the healthy bones of a single Pomeranian musketeer. I have sought to emphasise that we must be more sparing with the blood of our people and our soldiers when it is a question of deliberately embarking on a policy in which no interest of ours is involved . . .

From W.N. Medlicott and D.K. Coveney (eds.): *Bismarck and Europe* (1971)

Confederation to Empire

I Territorial changes in the Balkans 1875–78

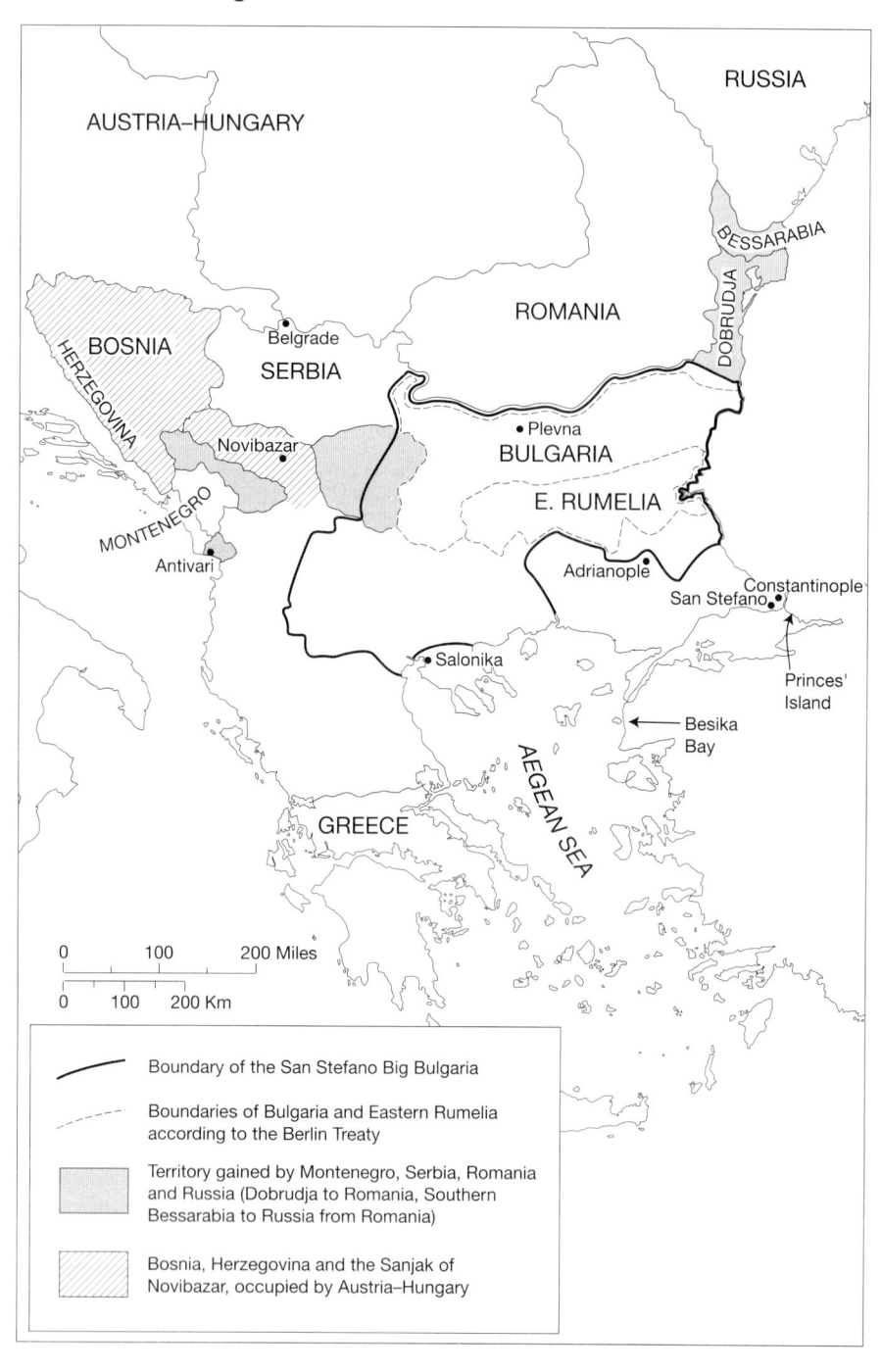

J Bismarck disappoints both the Austrians and the Russians at the Congress of Berlin

(i) Austrian reactions (from the notes of Baron Schwegel)

Bismarck will certainly have declared to the Russians that he attaches greater importance to the gratification of our wishes than those of England – at the moment he is strikingly, even demonstrably, friendly with Andrassy; but I do not trust him and I am convinced that basically he is only working for the Russians ... (22 May 1878)

Bismarck pleads illness and would like to go to Kissingen; but perhaps this is only a manoeuvre to help the Russians, whose gain will be all the greater, the more quickly and superficially everything is settled ... (26 June)

Prince Bismarck will press ruthlessly in the Congress for a rapid conclusion, as he wants first to go to Kissingen and then to Gastein, and be back here by 9 September, for the opening of the new *Reichstag* ... (2 July)

(ii) Russian reactions (from a Russian Foreign Office source on 7 June 1878)

You may well ask why we have so far not obtained any better results backed by the powerful goodwill of Bismarck. It is because we have been confronted by systematic opposition from England and Austria. Andrassy, very cordial, acting the gentleman in his talks with me, becomes a different person when in the presence of the English, and turns into a servile admirer of every word that falls from the lips of Beaconsfield. The consequence is that Bismarck, whose chief preoccupation is to avoid clashes, and to bring the Congress to an end, finds himself forced to tack between the three of them and does not always exert an energetic goodwill towards us ...

From W.N. Medlicott and D.K. Coveney (eds.): *Bismarck and Europe* (1971)

K Tsar Alexander II's 'Box-on-the-ears' letter (to William I of Germany on 3 August 1879)

... the Turks, sustained by their friends the English and Austrians, who in the meantime firmly hold two Turkish provinces, invaded by them in times of peace, and never to be returned to their legitimate sovereign, do not cease to raise difficulties of detail which are of the greatest importance as much for the Bulgars as for the brave Montenegrins. – The Rumanians will do the same vis-à-vis Bulgaria. – Decision rests with the majority of the European commissioners. Those of France and Italy join ours on practically all questions, while those of Germany appear to have received the word of command to support the Austrian view which is systematically hostile to us and is so in questions which in no way interest Germany but are very important for us.

Forgive, my dear Uncle, the frankness of my language based on the facts, but I think it my duty to call your attention to the sad consequences which these may cause in our good neighbourly relations by embittering our two nations against each other, as the press of the two countries is already doing. – I see in it the work of our common enemies, those who cannot stomach the alliance of the three emperors . . .

From W.N. Medlicott and D.K. Coveney (eds.): *Bismarck and Europe* (1971)

L   Britain's response to Bismarck's policies, relayed to Bismarck on 27 September 1879 by the German Ambassador in Britain

After I had told him in a few words the purpose of my visit, and had been assured of the fullest discretion and secrecy, Lord Beaconsfield began our conversation by telling me that he had thought a great deal about the present situation in Europe; he could not deny that he saw with a certain satisfaction that Russia, blinded and dominated by quite senseless Panslavism, was repelling her old ally and apparently abandoning the Three Emperors' Alliance, which had been of essential value to her. England must have and wished to have allies in order to play a part in European affairs; the policy of non-intervention was impracticable . . . The most natural allies for England were Germany and Austria. *He would enter joyfully into an alliance with Germany.* The main problem involved was France and the possibility of a Franco-Russian alliance. But he could give me on this very point the most solid assurances. France would never attack Germany as long as she saw that England would treat this attack as a *casus belli* . . .

From W.N. Medlicott and D.K. Coveney (eds.): *Bismarck and Europe* (1971)

M   The terms of the Dual Alliance, signed between the Austrian and German Empires, 7 October 1879

Article I. Should, contrary to their hope, and against the loyal desire of the two High Contracting Parties, one of the two Empires be attacked by Russia, the High Contracting Parties are bound to come to the assistance one of the other with the whole war strength of their Empires, and accordingly only to conclude peace together and upon mutual agreement.
Article II. Should one of the High Contracting Parties be attacked by another Power, the other High Contracting Party binds itself hereby, not only not to support the aggressor against its high Ally, but to observe at least a benevolent neutral attitude towards its fellow Contracting Party. Should, however, the attacking party in such a case be supported by Russia, either by an active cooperation or by military measures which constitute a menace to the Party attacked, then the obligation stipulated

Bismarck's Foreign Policy 1871–90

in Article I of this Treaty, for reciprocal assistance with the whole fighting force, becomes equally operative, and the conduct of the war by the two High Contracting Parties shall in this case also be in common until the conclusion of a common peace.
Article IV. This Treaty shall, in conformity with its peaceful character, and to avoid any misinterpretation, be kept secret by the two High Contracting Parties, and only communicated to a third Power upon a joint understanding between the two Parties, and according to the terms of a special Agreement.

From W.N. Medlicott and D.K. Coveney (eds.): *Bismarck and Europe* (1971)

N Bismarck tries to improve Austro-Russian relations, as reported by the Austrian Foreign Minister, Haymerle, to Franz Joseph on 9 September 1880

My two days' stay in Friedrichsruh was used almost exclusively by Prince Bismarck to advocate a better understanding with Russia and to support the wish of the Emperor Alexander that the triple agreement should be maintained, particularly with reference to the question of Bulgarian unification . . .

Prince Bismarck finds mistrust very understandable, he himself will not be lacking in caution; and thus, against the wishes of the military, he is insisting that the newly organised bodies of troops should be stationed, not on the western but on the eastern boundary, since Russia does not propose making any changes in the disposition of her troops in Poland. But he did not intend to show any mistrust, as it would not help the situation and would only bring Russia and England closer together. The republican movement in western Europe was making undeniable progress, not only in France, but especially in England, thanks to the foolish policy of Gladstone.

And so in the interests of the monarchical principle it was a question, not of loosening the ties between the three empires, but of strengthening them.

To bring about the revival of the Emperors' Alliance would be the only way to reawaken in England the sense of her true interests and to overthrow Gladstone which he considered to be one of the chief aims of his policy . . .

From W.N. Medlicott and D.K. Coveney (eds.): *Bismarck and Europe* (1971)

O Bismarck reassures the Russians (from the memoirs of Peter Alexandrovich Saburov, the Russian Ambassador in Berlin, 1880)

I expressed the opinion that Haymerle did not perhaps wish to enter into our plans, seeing that he believed Austria to be sufficiently protected by the Treaty of Alliance with Germany . . . The Prince answered me with a certain animation: 'Austria would be much mistaken, if she thought herself completely protected by us. I can assure you that this is not the case. Our interest orders us not to let Austria be *destroyed*, but she is not guaranteed against an attack. A war between Russia and Austria would place us, it is true, in a most embarrassing position, but our attitude in such circumstances will be dictated by our own interest and not by engagements which do not exist. Our interest demands that neither Russia nor Austria should be *completely* crippled. Their existence as Great Powers is equally necessary to us. That is what will guide our conduct in such an event.'

I inferred from these words that in the event of war, Germany is not unconditionally bound by an offensive and defensive alliance, but that it reserved the right to intervene, whether after the first battles, or in the peace negotiations ...

From W.N. Medlicott and D.K. Coveney (eds.): *Bismarck and Europe* (1971)

P Bismarck writes to William I in 1881 about the renewal of the *Dreikaiserbund*

As the Emperor Alexander is known to be a man who keeps his word, we may look on the peace of our two neighbours as assured for some years to come. Moreover, the danger for Germany of a Franco-Russian coalition is completely removed, and thereby the peaceful attitude of France towards us as good as guaranteed; at the same time as a result of the assurance that the young Emperor has given, the ground will be taken from under the feet of the anti-German war party in Russia, who have been trying to influence his decisions.

I have no doubt that after the lapse of three years, which is to be the initial duration of the treaty, it will be possible to achieve a further extension of this treaty for all three Imperial Courts, but in any case for Germany and Russia. I can therefore respectfully recommend to your Majesty the acceptance of the agreement made between the two other Imperial Courts.

From W.N. Medlicott and D.K. Coveney (eds.): *Bismarck and Europe* (1971)

Q Bismarck authorises the conclusion of the Triple Alliance, in a letter from the Under-Secretary of State to Reuss, the German ambassador in Vienna, 16 March 1882

Concerning your esteemed report no. 112 of 10th inst., the Chancellor remarked that it was not his intention to propose any formula for the agreement with Italy, which is directed exclusively against France. He only wanted to emphasise that in fact Italy was threatened first and foremost by France, and that therefore a mere treaty of neutrality or an agreement which offers no security against a French attack could not satisfy the needs of Italy. The Chancellor therefore begs Your Excellency to tell Kalnoky that he, for his part, would have no objection to a general formula in the agreement, especially as in the present circumstances Russia seems to be ahead of France on the slippery path to war.

With reference to Count Kalnoky's statement that Austria has nothing to fear from France, the Chancellor thinks that this does not accord with history. If Austria is involved in war with Russia and Germany is dragged in, the danger that France would turn against both Germany *and* Austria would not be remote.

From W.N. Medlicott and D.K. Coveney (eds.): *Bismarck and Europe* (1971)

R   Bismarck expresses German colonial demands in a letter to Münster, the German ambassador in London, dated 5 May 1884

I am delighted that our friendly attitude finds approval with Lord Granville. In accordance with His Majesty's wishes we are ready to win further approval, if the English for their part, show any signs of reciprocity.

They would have an opportunity for this first of all in considering our complaints about the use of force against German citizens in the Pacific, and in greater regard for our commercial interests in Africa.

We are of the opinion that foreign trade in all regions, which are not, beyond all doubt and by general recognition, directly annexed by a European power, should be open equally to all nations, and that further expansion of certain powers, as for example the one envisaged for Portugal by the Anglo-Portuguese treaty, could only take place under the generally accepted condition that the continuation and extension of *existing* trade connections should remain unaffected. Only if this concession were guaranteed by treaty would we recognise new seizures of territory by other powers. The Anglo-Portuguese treaty differs from this proviso in that it places under Portugal's very exclusive colonial rule distant coastal regions hitherto not dominated by her.

From W.N. Medlicott and D.K. Coveney (eds.): *Bismarck and Europe* (1971)

S   Bismarck's terms for colonial cooperation with France conveyed to Hatzfeldt, a German diplomat, on 7 August 1884

I wish to have news of the state of the negotiations regarding the regulation of west African trade relations similar to those for Eastern Asia. The present moment, after the breakdown of the London Conference, will be especially opportune for entrusting Prince Hohenlohe with overtures in Paris which, although confidential, will bring the negotiations practically nearer. If France seems willing for this, we could propose the drafting of an agreement together, by the terms of which freedom of trade with the coastal strips hitherto under European jurisdiction would be guaranteed

Confederation to Empire

for the participants in the treaty. As soon as we are agreed with France over the basic principles to be formulated on the lines of [those for] East Asia, we could then together invite the other interested powers, such as England, Holland, Spain, Portugal, Belgium (or one of the last two, if they have not reached an understanding with one another) to join, and provisionally try to make a settlement with those who are willing for it. If England can be persuaded to join, it would be very desirable, but I do not think it likely; on the contrary I believe that the exclusive English efforts to achieve supreme domination in extra-European waters will force the other trading nations to set up their own organisation as a counterpoise to English colonial supremacy.

From W.N. Medlicott and D.K. Coveney (eds.): *Bismarck and Europe* (1971)

T A possible motive for Bismarck's colonial policy – the Chancellor's son, Herbert, in 1890

When we entered upon a colonial policy, we had to reckon with a long reign of the Crown Prince. During this reign English influence would have been dominant. To prevent this we had to embark on a colonial policy because it was popular and consequently adapted to bring us into conflict with England at any given moment.

From Sebastian Haffner: *Germany's Self-destruction* (1989)

U Bismarck stresses the importance of Russo-German friendship in the *Reichstag* on 11 January 1887

Addressing the German *Reichstag*, Bismarck, after quoting Hamlet's remark, 'What's Hecuba to him?' continued: What's Bulgaria to us? It is a matter of complete indifference to us who rules in Bulgaria, and what becomes of Bulgaria – and that I repeat. I repeat everything that I said earlier when I used that expression, so much misused and ridden to death since, about the bones of a Pomeranian grenadier: in the whole Eastern question there is no question of war for us. No one is going to embroil us with Russia. ['Bravo!' on the right] Russia's friendship means more to us than that of Bulgaria and all the friends of Bulgaria that we have with us in this country. [Laughter on the right]

The question as to how we shall stand with France in the future, I find less easy to answer ... is this epoch of frontier warfare with the French nation at an end, or is it not? You are as little able to answer that question as I am. I can only voice my own suspicions in this regard, and say that it is not at an end; this would need a change in the entire French character and the whole frontier situation.

On our side we have done everything to persuade the French to forget the past ...

From W.N. Medlicott and D.K. Coveney (eds.): *Bismarck and Europe* (1971)

V The terms of the Reinsurance Treaty, signed between the German and Russian Empires, 18 June 1887

Article I. If one of the high contracting Parties should find itself at war with a third Great Power, the other would maintain a benevolent neutrality, and would try to localise the conflict. This provision would not apply to a war against Austria or France resulting from an attack on one of these two Powers by one of the high contracting Parties.

Article II. Germany recognises the rights historically acquired by Russia in the Balkan peninsula, and particularly the legitimacy of her preponderant and decisive influence in Bulgaria and in Eastern Roumelia. The two Courts engage to admit no modification of the territorial status quo of the said peninsula without a previous agreement between them, and to oppose in due course every attempt to disturb this status quo, or to modify it without their consent.

Article III. The two Courts recognise the European and mutually obligatory character of the principle of the closing of the Straits of the Bosphorus and of the Dardanelles, founded on international law, confirmed by the treaties and summed up in the declaration of the Second Plenipotentiary of Russia at the session of 12 July of the Congress of Berlin (protocol 19).

   They will ensure in common that Turkey shall make no exception to this rule in favour of the interests of any Government whatsoever, by lending to the warlike operations of a belligerent Power the portion of its Empire which forms the Straits. In case of infringement, or to prevent it if such infringement should be in prospect, the two Courts will inform Turkey that they would regard her, in this event, as putting herself in a state of war towards the injured party, and as depriving herself thenceforth of the benefits of the security assured to her territorial status quo by the Treaty of Berlin.

Article IV. The present Treaty shall remain in force for the space of three years from the day of the exchange of ratifications.

From W.N. Medlicott and D.K. Coveney (eds.): *Bismarck and Europe* (1971)

W The contradictions of Bismarck's policy, highlighted in a private letter from the Austrian Foreign Minister, Kalnoky, on 18 August 1887

What does us most harm at the moment in the east is the attitude of Germany in the Bulgarian question. It is quite true, and Prince Reusz has confirmed this, that Prince Bismarck, faithful to his earlier attitude, supports the Russian plans concerning Bulgaria on Constantinople and has advised the Sultan to come to an understanding with Russia, that is, to lead the Russians back to Bulgaria. This does not surprise me, and I was convinced that Bismarck will not change his russophile attitude as far as Bulgaria is concerned. On the other hand I doubt whether he will do more than remain consistent in theory, but this is more than enough to jeopardise the influence of our group. It is not to be wondered at if this peculiar attitude of Germany vis-à-vis the Sultan is misunderstood and causes confusion and distrust. Only a short while ago Germany sided with us, Italy, and England against the action of France and Russia in the Egyptian question. A few weeks later Germany, together with France, supports the Russians in a course of action which is blatantly hostile to us. What will the Turks make of this, and is it to be wondered at if they conclude that reliable alliances are no longer to be had? And yet it would not be true to believe that our alliance with Germany has in any way been undermined – on the contrary, on the German side there is an even greater effort to foster and cherish this alliance as the only reliable prop and bastion against war and its advocates ... It must be because of the very vulnerable position of Germany between France and Russia that Bismarck keeps trying to separate Russia from France by showing favour to the Emperor Alexander in the Bulgarian question, in which he has such a personal interest ...

From W.N. Medlicott and D.K. Coveney (eds.): *Bismarck and Europe* (1971)

Questions

1. What light is thrown on Bismarck's reasons for fostering the *Dreikaiserbund* by Sources A, B and C? **(7 marks)**
2. Using Sources D, E and F, explain why there was a 'War Scare' in 1875. **(6 marks)**
3. How far do Sources H, I and J explain why neither the Austrian nor the Russian governments were satisfied with Bismarck's policies in relation to the Balkans between 1876 and 1878? **(7 marks)**
4. Using your own knowledge and Sources K, L and M, explain why Bismarck concluded the Dual Alliance with the Austrian Empire in 1879. **(9 marks)**
5. Judging from the evidence of Sources N, O, P and Q, would you agree that in the early 1880s Bismarck was more concerned with isolating France than in cementing good relations with Russia? **(8 marks)**
6. What was Bismarck's motivation, as indicated in Sources R, S and T, for pursuing policies of colonial growth in the mid-1880s? **(6 marks)**
7. Using your own knowledge and Sources U, V and W, explain the contradictions in Bismarck's foreign policy in the 1880s. **(9 marks)**

7 WILLIAM II'S INTERNAL POLICIES 1890–1914

Leo, Count von Caprivi, was selected by William II to succeed Bismarck as Chancellor in the belief that he would be compliant to the Kaiser's wishes [A]. Initially the new government pursued progressive social policies, designed to conciliate the working classes; the anti-socialist laws were allowed to lapse. In 1892 Caprivi introduced tariff reforms, reducing the duties on food, which pleased the workers and industrialists but alarmed the Junkers – the landowning conservatives [B]. Caprivi also attempted to increase the size of the army [C], but this measure was defeated in the *Reichstag*. Consequently, in 1893, the *Reichstag* was dissolved and in the ensuing election the Social Democrats (*SPD*) won 44 seats. This alarmed William II who now urged the introduction of fresh anti-socialist legislation, a proposal rejected by Caprivi who resigned in 1894.

Under his successor, Hohenlohe, a 'policy of concentration' was introduced, aimed at winning the support of the middle classes for the crown, while at the same time attempts were made to deal with the apparent revolutionary threat posed by the *SPD* [D, E]. William II and his advisers failed to recognise that the party was by no means united in pursuing a revolutionary programme [F]. In any case, whatever policies were followed by succeeding governments, support for the socialists continued to grow [G].

In the period 1893 to 1914 the pace of industrial development in Germany increased almost without interruption [H]. Nevertheless this was not identified as an unqualified benefit [I]. Some right-wing conservatives saw only the threat posed by increasing numbers of socialist workers, and therefore urged that violent measures should be taken to protect the state [J]. However, Tirpitz, Secretary of State for the Navy, and his allies in the Navy League advocated a 'more constructive policy' – the building of a strong navy which would provide benefits for both industrialists and for many workers by security of employment [K, L]. The first Navy Law was passed in 1898 and Tirpitz ensured that a continuous naval building programme remained a priority until 1912 [M] (see also Chapter 8).

Believing that Hohenlohe was too cautious, William II replaced him as Chancellor in 1900 with Bernhard von Bülow. In 1902 Bülow, who had been intensely critical of Caprivi, introduced new tariff laws increasing the duty on imported grain, a move designed to please the conservative landowners [N]. By this time the German Empire was facing mounting financial problems, but the parties in the *Reichstag* disagreed on how taxes should be raised to pay for the country's military and social expenditure [O, P].

In 1908, William II allowed his views on Anglo-German relations to be published in the British newspaper the *Daily Telegraph*. This produced a storm of protest in Germany. When Bülow failed to defend the Kaiser's actions in the *Reichstag* [Q] William II determined to dismiss him. Exploiting Bülow's failure to solve the country's financial problems, the Kaiser replaced him with Theobald von Bethmann-Hollweg in 1909 [R]. Unfortunately for the new Chancellor, the Empire's internal position showed no signs of improvement. The army was an essential feature of the state [S] yet the increasing naval expenditure meant that it had been comparatively neglected [T]. There was continuous pressure to increase its size, but many in the military establishment feared that this could create new social difficulties [U], with more recruits coming from the industrial working classes and more officers from the bourgeoisie [V]. The result of the 1912 election with the *SPD* emerging as the largest party in the *Reichstag* seemed increasingly to threaten the stability of the Empire.

For many right-wing conservatives there were only two possible solutions [W], either a coup by the Kaiser [X] or a victorious war. German press reports in 1914 seemed to herald the adoption of the second solution [Y]. The failure of William II's governments to solve the internal problems of the German Empire had helped to push the country towards war in August 1914 [Z].

A The political instability of William II, revealed by Baron Holstein, a German Foreign Office official, in 1891

I am curious to see how long the present regime will survive. I do not put much reliance on the Kaiser's constancy ... Let us hope he will reach maturity before there is any serious testing time. In any case if we don't want a Republic we must take our princes as Providence sends them.

From Alan Palmer: *The Kaiser* (1978)

B Caprivi's tariff reforms

Our agriculture needs a protective tariff. Imported agricultural products must have a sufficiently heavy duty imposed on them to prevent the foreign supply from falling below a price at which our home agriculture can make a fair profit. The reduction of agrarian duties at the time of Caprivi's commercial policy brought about a crisis in our agriculture which it was only able to weather by dint of working with stubborn energy, and hoping for a complete change of tariff arrangements within a short time. If we sacrificed the protective tariff on agricultural products

William II's Internal Policies 1890–1914

in order to lower the cost of living by means of cheap imports, the danger would arise that agricultural work would grow more and more unprofitable, and would have to be given up to a greater and greater extent. We should go the way England has gone.

From Bernhard von Bülow: *Imperial Germany* (1914)

C   Chancellor Caprivi writes in April 1892 about the problems of increasing the size of the army

There is no doubt that, unless a partial concession is made to the desire for annual establishment of the peace-time strength and the legal introduction of two-year service, a strengthening of the army is not to be attained. To conflict, dissolution, or even *coup d'état* we dare not allow it to come. The question is not whether the three-year service in itself is preferable to two-year service, but whether we will give up the three-year service in order to increase our peacetime strength by 77 500 men ... Any attempt to carry the increase through without introducing two-year service can lead only to defeat which must weaken the Emperor's government within the *Reich* and abroad.

From Gordon Craig: *Germany 1866–1945* (1978)

D   The threat posed by the socialists

This organisation of the Social Democrats is definitely hostile to our political system, and looks on this hostility as its bond of union. There is no possibility of reconciling them to the State and of dissolving them in so doing, by tying them for a time to the Government cart, or allowing this member or the other to take part in the direction of affairs. The movement is far too strong to allow itself, so to speak, to be coupled like a truck to the Government locomotive, and to let itself be pulled along a definite track; it would want to be a locomotive itself, and would try to pull in the opposite direction. The Social Democrats would not obey a man from their midst who, in existing circumstances, should take service as a Minister any more than any other German party has ever done.

From Bernhard von Bülow: *Imperial Germany* (1914)

E   The Marxist–Socialist view – August Bebel, the Socialist party leader, 1903

I want to remain the deadly enemy of this bourgeois society and this political order in order to undermine it in its conditions of existence and, if I can, to eliminate it entirely.

From William Carr: *A History of Germany 1815–1990* (1991)

Confederation to Empire

F The revisionist-socialist view of Eduard Bernstein, *SPD* leader, in 1899

Constitutional legislation works more slowly. Its path is usually that of compromise, not the prohibition but the buying out of acquired rights. But it is stronger than the revolution scheme where prejudice and the limited horizon of the great mass of the people appear as hindrance to social progress, and it offers greater advantages where it is the question of the creation of permanent economic arrangements capable of lasting; in other words, it is best adopted to positive social-political work. In legislation intellect dominates over emotion in quiet times; during a revolution emotion dominates over intellect.

From Albert Fried and Ronald Sanders (eds.): *Socialist Thought* (1964)

G The increase in support for the Social Democratic Party
(i) The increase in votes for the party

Year	Votes
1884	550 000
1887	763 000
1890	1 427 000
1893	1 787 000
1898	2 107 000
1903	3 011 000
1907	3 539 000
1912	4 250 000

(ii) The increase in seats in the *Reichstag*

Year	Seats
1884	24
1887	11
1890	35
1893	44
1898	56
1903	81
1907	43
1912	110

From Bernhard von Bülow: *Imperial Germany* (1914)

H German economic growth

The number of persons employed in commerce and industry is continually on the increase, as is the number of large undertakings. The rapid growth of general prosperity, chiefly due to industry and commerce, is quite obvious. To take one example from among many, the official statistics in the year 1909 report 4579 commercial companies with a capital of 15 860 million marks, which pay yearly dividends to the amount of about 1000 million ... And following the development of foreign trade, the German mercantile marine increased (in 1000 gross registered tonnage) from 2650 in 1900 to 4267 in 1909, and 4467 in 1911. In the German shipyards the construction of ships, including river craft and warships, rose from 385 in 1900 to 814 in 1909 and 859 in 1911 ... In the year 1882, agriculture still employed almost as many men as commerce and industry together; in the year 1895 the number of its employees was less by almost 2 000 000 than those of industry alone. In thirteen years a complete change of conditions had eventuated.

From Bernhard von Bülow: *Imperial Germany* (1914)

I The dangers of industrial growth – the Secretary to the Treasury writing in 1896
Germany is becoming more and more an industrial state. Thereby that part of the population is strengthened upon which the crown cannot depend – the population of the great towns and industrial districts, whereas the agricultural population provided the real support of the monarchy. If things went on as at present, then the monarchy would either pass to a republican system or, as in England, become a sham monarchy.

From V.R. Berghahn: *Germany and the Approach of War in 1914* (1973)

J General Alfred von Waldersee gives his advice to William II in 1897 on how to deal with the threat of the socialists
In view of the tremendous growth of the Social Democrat movement it appears to me to be inevitable that we are approaching the moment when the state's instruments of power must measure themselves with those of the working masses ... But if the struggle is inevitable ... the state cannot gain anything from postponing it. I feel that it is in the state's interest not to leave it to the Social Democrat leaders to decide when the great reckoning is to begin; rather it should do everything possible to force an early decision. For the moment the state is, with certainty, still strong enough to suppress any rising.

From V.R. Berghahn: *Germany and the Approach of War in 1914* (1973)

K The reasons for a continuous battleship building programme
(i) Prince Otto zu Salm, President of the Navy League, writing to Tirpitz in 1901
The ordering of new warships would stimulate trade and industry. This in turn would push stockmarket prices up, save many assets and bring about a consolidation of the economy.
(ii) Admiral von Tirpitz, writing in November 1905
For the navy, however, the ratification of a (fixed) organisational

structure would, as such, not represent a gain. By refusing to replace ships, the *Reichstag* can in fact immobilise the navy. Only through a legally binding clause fixing the replacement of ships can the navy gain a similar stability as the army possesses. As the earlier (pre-1898) period has shown, the *Reichstag* disposes ever great powers vis-à-vis the *Reich*'s government [because of its] annual appropriation of ships.

From V.R. Berghahn: *Germany and the Approach of War in 1914* (1973)

L   A modern assessment of Tirpitz's programme

Tirpitz came to the Naval Office with a well thought out, comprehensive naval construction programme. The creation of a mammoth battle fleet would provide the basis for a great overseas policy. This, in turn, would mean large building contracts and hence prosperity for German industry and proletariat alike. Boom and profits would buttress at home the dominant political and social position of the ruling elements and, it was hoped, arrest demands for parliamentarisation on the part of the Social Democrats and the Liberals, and at the same time would turn the energies of Germany's middle classes towards overseas expansion.

From H.H. Herwig: *Luxury Fleet: the Imperial German Navy 1888–1918* (1980)

M   Industrial motives for maintaining the shipbuilding programme – from the diary of the Conservative politician, Zedlitz, in April 1909

Well-known enthusiasts apart, there are quite a few influential people here who are opposed to any limitation of armaments. It would be very interesting to learn something about the various connections which exist between the fleet fanatics and the manufacturers of the fleet. The power of the steel kings weighs heavily, and the worry about their business, the desire to keep the share index high has frequently been served to us as a national concern.

From V.R. Berghahn: *Germany and the Approach of War in 1914* (1973)

N   The reasons for the 1902 Tariff Law

Owing to a momentary standstill in exports the Caprivi–Marschall Tariff Policy was directed entirely towards commercial treaties. In order to be able to conclude favourable commercial treaties as easily and rapidly as possible, foreign countries were offered a reduction in the duty on corn. But the opinion of clever business men, that the demands of the other parties increase in proportion as they are offered more, proved to be right in the end. The important commercial treaty with Russia, who derived great advantages from the reduction in the duties on cereals, was only concluded after negotiations which lasted three full years and were interrupted by a tariff war. Agriculture had to pay for the commercial treaties, since it had for the space of 12 years to work under considerably less favourable conditions, owing to the reduction in the corn tax from 5 to $3\frac{1}{2}$ marks.

Thanks to the Tariff Law of 1902, our economic policy regained that agrarian bias so indispensable to the interests of the whole community. Side by side with the foreign trade, advancing with such mighty strides, the maintenance of a strong home industry was secured. German agriculture, under the influence of the new tariff and of the commercial treaties based on it, has experienced a decade of vigorous development. Our robust and hardworking farmers recovered the feeling that the Empire had an interest in the success of their work; that it no longer looked upon agriculture as an industrial stepchild, but as one having equal rights and, indeed, as the first-born of its mother Germania.

From Bernhard von Bülow: *Imperial Germany* (1914)

O The financial state of the *Reich*, reported to the *Reichstag* by Bülow in 1905

The finances of the *Reich* have gradually fallen into a state that requires speedy and thoroughgoing correction. The *Reich*'s burden of debt has, because of lack of systematic amortisation [the reduction of debt by regularly putting money into a sinking fund], steadily increased. The finances of the federal states are suffering heavily because of the increased claims that the *Reich* makes on them. The nation's new cultural and political responsibilities are awaiting upon the solution of this problem. It is incontrovertible that the *Reich* is in need of new income.

From Gordon Craig: *Germany 1866–1945* (1978)

P The continuing financial problem – the Secretary to the Treasury writing to Tirpitz in August 1909

The internal structure of the *Reich*, its defence capabilities and its external prestige demand not merely a standstill, but an energetic reduction of expenditure, [otherwise] the development will end inescapably in the complete collapse of our finances and all national activities stemming from them.

From V.R. Berghahn: *Germany and the Approach of War in 1914* (1973)

Q Bülow fails to defend the Kaiser in the *Reichstag* over the *Telegraph* interview 1908

The knowledge that the publication ... has caused much excitement and pain in our country will induce His Majesty henceforth to maintain even in his private conversation that reserve which is equally essential for coherent government policy and for the authority of the Crown.

From Alan Palmer: *The Kaiser* (1978)

Confederation to Empire

R   Bülow's dismissal – the assessment of a recent historian
Bülow had long been conscious that the Bismarckian system of government was ill-suited to an empire of 60 million subjects, which was by now the leading industrial power in Europe. Tentatively he began to propose reforms. But the old-guard Prussian conservatives would surrender none of their privileges. Bülow wanted to impose death duties on the great estates; the Junkers saw no reason to balance the budget at their expense; and by mid-summer the Chancellor's *Reichstag* majority had melted away. This was the opportunity for which William had waited ever since Bülow's treachery during the *Daily Telegraph* debate. On 29 June 1909 Bülow travelled to Kiel and, in an audience aboard the *Hohenzollern* [the Imperial yacht] formally resigned the chancellorship.

From Alan Palmer: *The Kaiser* (1978)

S   William II and the army
(i)   William II, in his accession speech, 1889
We are bound to each other – I and the army – we are born for each other, and we shall hold together indissolubly whether it be God's will to send us calm or storm.

(ii)   William II, in a speech to the royal guards, November 1891
You have sworn loyalty to me, children of my guard, and that means that you are now my soldiers, you have given yourselves to me, body and soul. The only enemy you have is now my enemy. With the present subversive activities of the socialists it could come about that I order you to shoot down your own relations, brothers, even your parents. God forbid that this should happen, but in the event you must obey your orders without a word.

From Giles MacDonagh: *Prussia, The Perversion of an Idea* (1995)

T   Difficulties for the army, expressed by a friend of the Kaiser in 1903
The army has become the castle guard and has to do sentry-go because we have not even yet contrived to win the hearts of the people.

From V.R. Berghahn: *Germany and the Approach of War in 1914* (1973)

U   The Prussian Minister of War writes to Chancellor Bethmann-Hollweg in 1910 about the political problem of increasing the size of the army
The last occasion when the army establishment was fixed was through the law ... of 25.3.1899. I do not have to explain to Your Excellency the reasons for this which, military considerations apart, belong to the

realm of politics and are connected also with the international reputation of the *Reich*.

From V.R. Berghahn: *Germany and the Approach of War in 1914* (1973)

V A later assessment of the importance of the officer caste in William II's Germany

Clearly the military establishment of the Prusso-German monarchy cannot be separated from the rest of society. Yet there is equally little doubt that the powerful officer corps was intimately connected and interwoven with a small minority which wielded an excess of political, economic and social power. It is not surprising that this élite ... should try to preserve its privileged position in society at large against the pressure for greater popular participation and that, in view of the great political weight of the officer corps within the power structure, military values should tend to influence the formation of basic policies.

From V.R. Berghahn: *Germany and the Approach of War in 1914* (1973)

W The *Frankfurter Zeitung* reports on the state of the German Empire in 1914

The social tensions are growing and so is the gaping gulf between heavy industry and the finished goods industry, between the beneficiaries of our economic policy and those who are disadvantaged by it, between the propertied and the propertyless classes, between capital and labour. And the trend is that this gulf will become even bigger.

From V.R. Berghahn: *Germany and the Approach of War in 1914* (1973)

X William II's solutions to Germany's problems, as perceived by Chancellor Bethmann-Hollweg in 1913

The idea that he will ally himself with the Princes in order to chastise the *Reichstag* and eventually abolish it, or will send one of his adjutant generals into the *Reichstag*, if I am not tough enough, constantly crops up in conversation with me.

From Paul Kennedy: *The Rise of Anglo-German Antagonism 1860–1914* (1982)

Y The German press and the prospects of war
(i) The Social Democrat newspaper *Vorwärts*, 1914

For many years, one declared a war between Germany and England to be inevitable and demanded year after year a strengthening of the fleet. Now Russia is turned into an aggressive enemy. The armaments industry always needs a bugbear to generate the necessary anxiety in which even the maddest claims are granted.

(ii) *Frankfurter Zeitung*, 4 March 1914
Broad circles of the population have allowed themselves to be seized by a nervousness which offers the armaments enthusiasts and war fanatics the fertile soil into which to put the seeds of new army increases.

(iii) The ultra-conservative *Ostpreussiche Zeitung*, December 1912
A fresh and uninhibited war would immediately decimate the 110 Social Democrats in the *Reichstag*.

From Paul Kennedy: *The Rise of Anglo-German Antagonism 1860–1914* (1982)

Z An overview of the internal policies of William II's governments
Imperial Germany's power structure entirely ruled out a socially egalitarian economic policy which would have promoted the well-being of the majority of her population. This has to be stated without hesitation for it is empirically irrefutable. It was the pre-industrial élites, such as the great landowners, the new barons of heavy industry, and, in particular, the political leaders of Germany's authoritarian government, who derived the greatest benefit from state interventionism in the long and short terms. At the same time, it was also the case that the 'artificial increase in the cost of living caused by tariffs' was one of the 'most effective means of creating massive unrest' which in turn increased 'the breeding ground of Social Democracy'.

From Hans-Ulrich Wehler: *The German Empire 1871–1918* (1985)

Questions

1. How far are the fears expressed by Waldersee in Source J substantiated by the evidence of Sources D to G? **(10 marks)**
2. In what ways do the arguments expressed by contemporaries in Sources K and M support the views of the historian H.H. Herwig as expressed in Source L? **(7 marks)**
3. Using your own knowledge and Sources O and P, examine the view that Germany's greatest internal problem after 1900 was how to finance the government's programmes. **(8 marks)**
4. How far do Sources S, T and V support the view that 'The army was the single most important element in the *Reich*'? **(8 marks)**
5. In what respects do Sources W, X and Y support the view that war was the inevitable solution to Germany's internal problems? **(8 marks)**

8 WILLIAM II'S FOREIGN POLICY: THE EARLY YEARS

Once Bismarck had been deprived of office, a 'New Course' was proclaimed in foreign policy – the maintenance of peace [A, B]. In practice the first significant act of policy was the non-renewal of the Reinsurance Treaty with Russia in 1890. In contrast to the expressed intentions of William II, Bismarck, writing in 1894, identified this as the adoption of a more adventurous policy [C]. One of the motives for abandoning the Reinsurance Treaty was a desire to improve relations with Britain [D], and in the same year Britain and Germany signed the 'Heligoland' treaty. Germany gave up her position in Zanzibar, limited her claims in East Africa and in return received the Island of Heligoland [E–G]. Caprivi, as Chancellor, was anxious to keep a friendly British government in office [H].

After the accession of Nicholas II to the throne of Russia in 1894, William II attempted to restore friendly relations with the Russian Empire on the basis of a personal relationship between the sovereigns [I]. Even as late as July 1905 when the two emperors met at Björkö in the Baltic on the German royal yacht, Nicholas II was persuaded to sign a defensive alliance against attack by any European power [J]. However, by the end of the year this had been abandoned by the Tsar in the interests of preserving good relations with France [K].

In the mid-1890s German foreign policy became increasingly aggressive [L, M]. Germany was determined to establish itself as a world power. 'The German *Reich* has become *"Weltreich"* [a world power]' declared William II. British public opinion was offended by the telegram [N] sent by the Kaiser to President Kruger of the Transvaal in January 1896 congratulating him on defeating the pro-British extremists who had crossed into the Transvaal hoping to incite an uprising against Kruger's government, an incident that became known as the Jameson Raid [O]. In the following year the policy of increasing Germany's world role was clearly indicated by the acquisition of the port-territory of Kiaochow in Northern China [P, Q]. In this same period England was increasingly identified as a potential enemy likely to resist German colonial expansion [R, S].

It was for this reason as well as the need to provide industrial development that Tirpitz argued in favour of the creation of a strong German navy [T], further worsening relations with Britain [U]. However, during the Anglo-Boer War (1899–1901) efforts were made, particularly by the British government [V, W], to rebuild friendly

Confederation to Empire

relations between the two countries. Initially the situation seemed favourable [X] but by 1901 hopes of an alliance were dead [Y].

Thus in the period after Bismarck's fall from power the German Empire had soured relations with Russia without the compensation of improved relations with Britain.

A The basis of William II's foreign policy (written in 1892)

I hope Europe will gradually come to realise the fundamental principle of my policy: leadership in the peaceful sense – a policy which gives expression to the force of arms – in the peaceful sense. I am of the opinion that it is already a success that I, having come to govern at an early age, stand at the head of German armed might yet have left my sword in its scabbard and have given up Bismarck's policy of eternally causing disruption to replace it with a peaceful foreign situation such as we have not known for many years. Slowly people will come to realise this.

From J.C.G. Roehl (ed.): *From Bismarck to Hitler* (1970)

B The peaceful intent of German foreign policy

Without boastfulness or exaggeration, we may say that never in the course of history has any Power, possessing such superior military strength as the Germans, served the cause of peace in an equal measure. This fact cannot be explained by our well-known and undoubted love of peace. The German has always been peace-loving, and has nevertheless had to draw his sword again and again in order to defend himself against foreign attacks. As a matter of fact, peace has primarily been preserved, not because Germany herself did not attack other nations, but because other nations feared a repulse in the event of their attacking Germany. The strength of our armaments has proved to be a more effective guarantee of peace than any in the last tumultuous centuries. An historical judgment is contained in this fact.

From Bernhard von Bülow: *Imperial Germany* (1914)

C Bismarck identifies dangers in the situation

If Germany has the advantage that her policy is free from direct interests in the East, on the other side is the disadvantage of the central and exposed position of the German Empire, with its extended frontier which has to be defended on every side, and the ease with which anti-German coalitions are made. At the same time Germany is perhaps the single Great Power in Europe which is not tempted by any objects which can only be attained by a successful war. It is our interest to maintain peace, while without exception our continental neighbours have wishes, either secret or officially avowed, which cannot be fulfilled except by war ... we must do our best to prevent war or limit it.

From Bismarck: *Reflections and Reminiscences 1891–1898* (1898)

D   A modern historian explains the abandonment of the Reinsurance Treaty

Part of the rationale for jettisoning the Reinsurance Treaty had been that, once rid of the embarrassing arrangement, the German government could create a healthier and more coherent system in which the junior partners in the Triple Alliance and the Danubian federates of that combination would feel a stronger obligation to accept German leadership and in which Great Britain, already associated since the Mediterranean Agreement of 1887, with Austria–Hungary and Italy, would be persuaded to give formal guarantees to protect the interests of those powers and eventually become a fully fledged member of the Triple Alliance.

From Gordon Craig: *Germany 1866–1945* (1978)

E   The importance of Heligoland to Germany – a telegram from the German Foreign Office to Count Hatzfeldt, German Ambassador in London, 29 May 1890

Telegram   **Secret**

You will note, as I mentioned in my telegram of May 25th, that the possession of Heligoland is of supreme importance to us and is by far the most serious matter in the whole negotiation. His Majesty shares the Chancellor's opinion that without Heligoland the Kiel Canal is useless to our Navy. We shall, therefore, always regard the acquisition of Heligoland as a gain in itself even as against the concessions mentioned in my telegram, or any other similar ones in the colonies.

You may point out to Lord Salisbury that you are convinced that so good an opportunity will scarcely occur twice for settling two questions so threatening to Anglo-German relations – East Africa and Heligoland – in a way which give so little cause of complaint to the jingoes [chauvinists] either in England or in Germany. No German Government can put off for ever public discussion of the question, why England attaches such disproportionate value to the possession of this islet, which has no importance in peace-time, but which makes the coast defence of Germany difficult, and facilitates hostile observation and attack.

German sense of fairness will appreciate the suggestion that no one can be called upon to give up a possession for nothing. Since up till now we have had nothing tangible to offer to England, it was easy to restrict discussion of the Heligoland question by the Press and the public within the narrow limits of casual mention. But now that we are ready to exchange certain territorial claims for Heligoland – claims, the mere raising of which appears serious enough to excite public opinion throughout England, the affair bears quite a different aspect. If at this point the exchange were refused by England, Germany would realise that no price would induce England to give up a possession, which is only important as a means of injuring Germany in the event of war.

From E.T.S. Dugdale (ed.): *German Diplomatic Documents 1871–1914* (1930)

F   Negotiations for the exchange of territory – a telegram from Hatzfeldt to the German Foreign Office, 30 May 1890
Telegram   **Secret**
I never forget the importance of Heligoland, but I should not recommend indicating its true importance too soon to Lord Salisbury, who *so far* regards Heligoland as in reality of no value *to us*. There would then be *no* further concession to be obtained in the colonies, and we should be obliged to grant *all* colonial demands, in order to gain the island.

At our last meeting, I for this reason did not begin about Heligoland but I left it for Lord Salisbury. At the end he said that he now wishes to discuss it with his colleagues, some of whom were *nervous* on the point on account of Parliament and public opinion. He did *not* share this view. I encouraged him in this and added that I hoped to secure for him the protectorate over Zanzibar in return.

From E.T.S. Dugdale (ed.): *German Diplomatic Documents 1871–1914* (1930)

William II's Foreign Policy: The Early Years

G The scramble for Africa

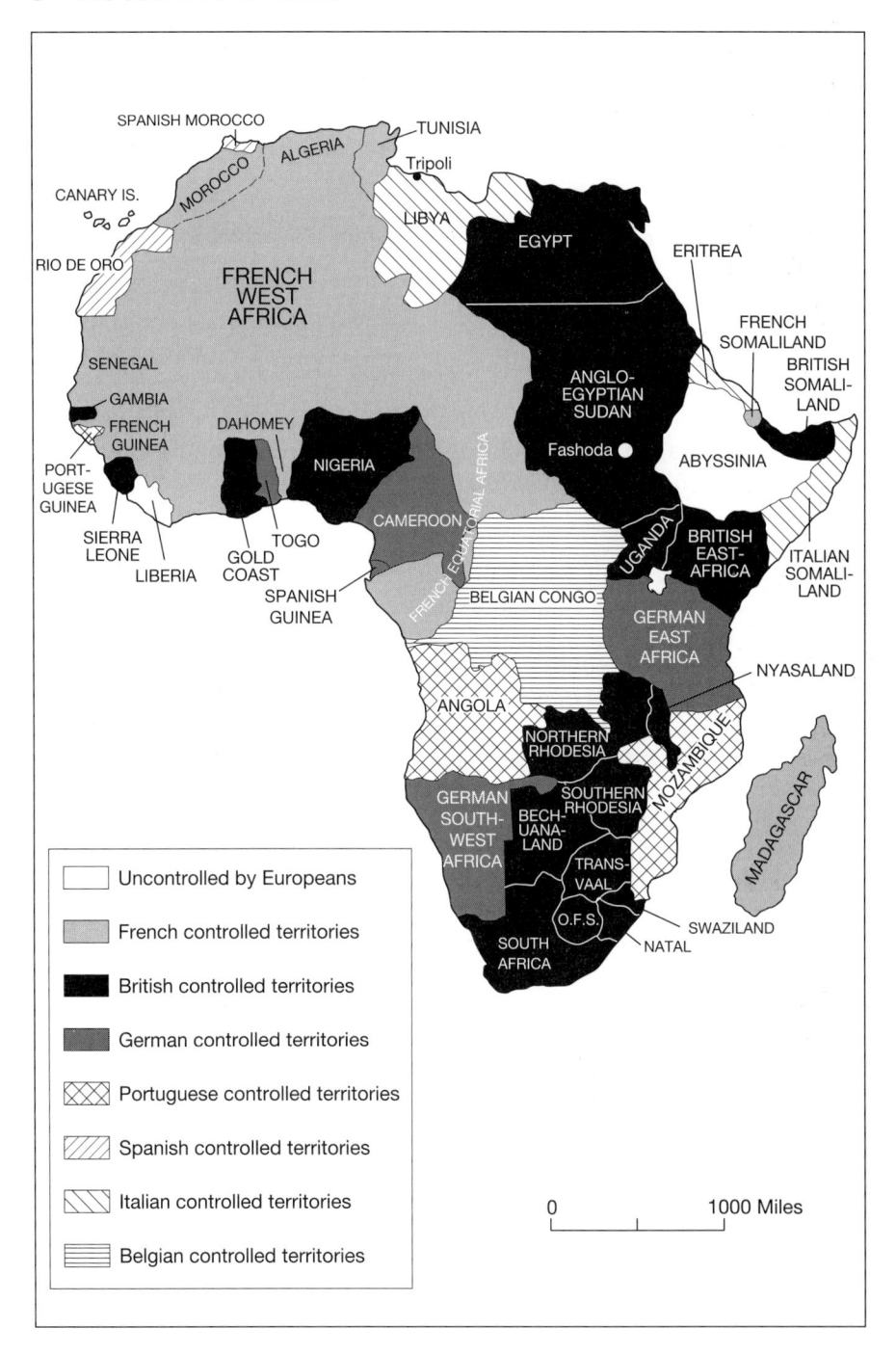

H Chancellor Caprivi notes in 1890 the importance of Salisbury's government staying in office

The position of the English government is not an easy one in view of the excited public opinion. Germany had to keep in mind the need to lighten Lord Salisbury's task and to make possible his retention of office.

From Paul Kennedy: *The Rise of Anglo-German Antagonism 1860–1914* (1982)

I The 'Willy–Nicky' correspondence – William II's letters to Nicholas II of Russia, 1895

26 April 1895

I shall certainly do all in my power to keep Europe quiet, and also guard the rear of Russia so that nobody shall hamper your action towards the Far East!
For that is clearly the great task of the future for Russia to cultivate the Asian Continent and to defend Europe from the inroads of the Great Yellow race. In this you will always find me on your side, ready to help you as best I can . . .

26 September 1895

The proposed new Corps would increase the overwhelming French forces to five Corps, and constitutes a threat as well as a serious danger to my country . . . [it] has made people uneasy here and given affairs an ugly look, as if Russia would like France to be offensive against Germany with the hopes of help from the first named . . . *I* perfectly know that *you* personally do not dream of attacking us, but still you cannot be astonished that the European Powers get alarmed seeing how the presence of your officers and high officials in an *official way* in France fans the inflammable [sic] Frenchman into a white heated passion and strengthens the cause of Chauvinism and Revanche! . . . if France goes on openly or secretly encouraged like this to violate all rules of international courtesy and Peace in peace times, one fine day my dearest Nicky you will find yourself *nolens volens* [willy-nilly] suddenly embroiled in the most horrible of wars Europe ever saw! . . .

25 October 1895

It is not a *fact* of the *Rapport* or friendship between Russia and France that makes one uneasy . . . but the danger which is brought to our Principle of Monarchism through the lifting up [of] the Republic on a pedestal by the form under which the friendship is shown. The constant appearance of Princes, Grand-dukes, statesmen, Generals in 'full fig' at reviews, burials, dinners, races, with the head of the Republic or in his entourage makes Republicains [sic] . . . believe that they are quite honest excellent people with whom Princes can consort and feel at home! . . . Don't forget that Jaurès . . . sits on the throne of the King and Queen of France 'by the Grace of God' whose heads Frenchmen

William II's Foreign Policy: The Early Years

Republicans cut off! The Blood of their Majesties is still on that country! Look at it, has it since then ever been happy or quiet again? Has it not staggered from bloodshed to bloodshed? And in its great moments did it not go from war to war? Till it soused all Europe and Russia in streams of blood? Till at last it had the Commune over again? Nicky take my word on it the curse of God has stricken that people forever!

If, unfortunately, as a result of a mature examination of the situation, Germany and Italy should both recognise that the maintenance of the status quo has become impossible, Germany engages, after a formal and previous agreement, to support Italy in any action in the form of occupation or other taking of guaranty which the latter should undertake in these same regions with a view to an interest of equilibrium and legitimate compensation.

It is understood that in such an eventuality the two Powers would seek to place themselves likewise in agreement with England.

From N.F. Grant: *The Kaiser's Letters to the Tsar* (1920)

J   William II describes the signing of the Björkö Treaty to Bülow, 1905
It was quiet as death; no sound but the waves, while the sun shone brightly into the dark cabin. I could just see the *Hohenzollern* gleaming white with its imperial standard fluttering in the breeze. I was just reading on the black cross the letters 'God with us' when I heard the Tsar's voice beside me saying (in English) 'That is quite excellent. I agree.' ... By God's grace this morning of July 24 1895 at Björkö is a turning point in Europe's history, a great burden has been lifted from my beloved Fatherland, which will at last be freed from terrible Gallo-Russian pincers ... God has ordained and willed it.

From Alan Palmer: *The Kaiser* (1978)

K   The failure of the Björkö Treaty
(i)   Nicholas II to William II, 7 October 1905
I think that the coming into force of the Björkö Treaty ought to be put off until we know how the French will look at it.
(ii)   Nicholas II to William II, 1905
Russia has no reasons to abandon her ally [France] nor suddenly to violate her.

From A.J.P. Taylor: *The Struggle for Mastery in Europe 1848–1918* (1954)

L   The aims of German foreign policy expressed in a Memorandum from Admiral Georg von Müller to the Kaiser's brother, 1896
World history is now dominated by the economic struggle. This struggle has raged over the whole globe but most strongly in Europe, where its nature is governed by the fact that central Europe (*Mittel-europa*) is

getting too small and that the free expansion of the peoples who live here is restricted as a result of the present distribution of the inhabitable parts of the earth and above all as a result of the world domination of England. These countries are threatened with further restrictions both in trading activity and in the opportunity of accommodating their surplus population in their own colonies, so to make use of them in a national way. The war which could – and many say must – result from this situation of conflict would according to the generally accepted opinion in our country have the aim of breaking England's world domination in order to lay free the necessary colonial possessions for the central European states who need to expand.

These states are the German *Reich*, Austria–Hungary and Italy. The Scandinavian countries and Switzerland could with some justice also be included. But Germany stands far ahead in the need and indeed the right to expand – a right which is surely established by what she has already achieved in the field of world trade.

From J.C.G. Roehl (ed.): *From Bismarck to Hitler* (1970)

M   The case for an aggressive foreign policy
(i)   A letter from Baron Holstein, Foreign Office official, 1897
The government of William II needs a tangible success abroad which will have an effect at home. This success can only come about as the result of a European War, a world historical gamble, or else some acquisition outside Europe.

(ii)   Herman Rehm, Professor of Law, Freiburg University, 1900
Only the idea of Germany as a world power is capable of dispelling the conflicts between rival economic interests in internal affairs.

From Hans-Ulrich Wehler: *The German Empire 1871–1918* (1985)

N   The Kruger Telegram – William II to President Kruger, 3 January 1896
I express my sincere congratulations that, supported by your people, without appealing for the help of friendly Powers, you have succeeded by your own energetic action against armed bands which invaded your country as disturbers of the peace, and have thus been enabled to restore peace and safeguard the independence of the country against attacks from the outside.

From E.T.S. Dugdale (ed.): *German Diplomatic Documents 1871–1914* (1930)

O   The reaction in England
(i)   A telegram from the German Foreign Office to Hatzfeldt in London, 6 January 1896
The British Ambassador mentioned today the unfavourable impression which His Majesty's telegram to President Kruger had made on British

public opinion. I replied that I must decidedly take exception to the view adopted by the British Press, that the telegram implied hostility to England and an invasion of her rights. In the matter of rights the German was very sensitive; he had no wish to infringe foreign rights, but he demanded that his own should be respected. It could not possibly be called an act of hostility to England for the German Emperor to congratulate the Head of a friendly State on having beaten armed bands, which had entered his country illegally and had been declared 'outlaws' by the British Government itself. Moreover, Germany had a right to speak of the independence of the South African Republic, since that had been recognised in the Convention concluded by England with that State in 1884, except for the minor restriction on Art. IV. I considered the British Press in the wrong in speaking of England's suzerainty over the South African Republic, after this had been formally and in essence removed by that Convention.

(ii) **A private message from Hatzfeldt to Holstein at the German Foreign Office, 7 January 1896**
Lord Salisbury was very friendly today and assured me emphatically that there was no fear of anything further being done against the Transvaal. His chief fear was that Jameson's life was in danger, as this, so he says, would make his task here immeasurably more difficult. He expressed no wish, but I have no doubt that he would be very grateful if we would suggest moderation to Herr Kruger, or at least advise him to wait. The very general and deep bitterness in the Press against us seems to be less today. I privately advised Lord Salisbury quietly to recommend the newspapers to abstain from further personal attacks on His Majesty, and he promised readily to do this.

   He said that he was not yet decided whether he ought not to give expression to the views held here in answer to the Secretary of State's assertion to Lascelles, that England could claim no suzerainty over the Transvaal. I advised him against it, explaining why the claim to real suzerainty could not be completely justified. He said finally that it was best to let the question rest and only to speak of the maintenance of the status quo, that being a subject on which both parties were agreed.

From E.T.S. Dugdale (ed.): *German Diplomatic Documents 1871–1914* (1930)

P   The seizure of Kiaochow – William II to Bülow, November 1897
Hundreds of German traders will be delighted to learn that the German Empire has at last gained a foothold in Asia; hundreds of thousands of Chinese will tremble when they feel the iron fist of Germany lying heavily on their neck; and the entire German people will rejoice that their government has taken firm action. Once and for all time I shall

show that the German Kaiser is no person with whom to take liberties nor to have as an enemy.

From Alan Palmer: *The Kaiser* (1978)

Q   The British reaction to the seizure of Kiaochow – a cipher telegram from Hatzfeldt to the German Foreign Office, 12 January 1898
Today Lord Salisbury again declared that no British interest would be injured by our settling down at Kiaochow ... He remarked that he had from the first objected not so much to the fact of our occupation of Kiaochow, as to the form in which it had been done, chiefly because he regarded it as a dangerous precedent, which *others* might imitate. I replied that I did not share this view and that no other way had been open to us, for the Chinese Government had clearly refused to understand that it was the duty of gratitude, as well as to their own interests to place at our disposal the coaling station, which will be indispensable to us in future; the Minister admitted that there was no other way of obtaining this object.

From E.T.S. Dugdale (ed.): *German Diplomatic Documents 1871–1914* (1930)

R   Increasing antagonism to Britain in Germany, as perceived by the Austro-Hungarian Ambassador in Berlin, 1896
The rivalry for world markets, opposing interests in their colonial policy, and the traditions of the Bismarckian political school, according to which England was portrayed as totally untrustworthy and often as perfidious, have prepared the terrain for hostile feeling towards England which has manifested itself here with unusual unanimity. In my opinion, it will be no easy task to convince influential circles that, in their own well-known interests, they must keep within limits in their stance against England.

From Paul Kennedy: *The Rise of Anglo-German Antagonism 1860–1914* (1982)

S   England seen as Germany's main potential enemy – Tirpitz in his first interview with William II, June 1897
For Germany the most dangerous enemy at the present time is England. It is also the enemy against which we most urgently require a certain measure of naval force as a political power factor ... our fleet must be so constructed that it can unfold its greatest military potential between Heligoland and the Thames ... The military situation against England demands battleships in as great a number as possible.

From Paul Kennedy: *The Rise of Anglo-German Antagonism 1860–1914* (1982)

William II's Foreign Policy: The Early Years

T   The chances of naval success against England
(i)   Tirpitz to William II, 1899
Thanks to our geographical position, our system of military service, mobilisation, torpedo-boats, tactical training, organisational structure [and] our uniform leadership by the monarch we shall no doubt have [a] good chance against England.

(ii)   Tirpitz to William II, September 1899
If one disregards our military position which is by no means hopeless, England will (after the completion of the German fleet) have lost, for general political reasons and because she will view the situation from the purely sober standpoint of a businessman, all inclination to attack us ... she will concede to Your Majesty such a measure of maritime influence which will make it possible for Your Majesty to conduct a good overseas policy.

From V.R. Berghahn: *Germany and the Approach of War in 1914* (1973)

U   The impact of German naval expansion of Anglo-German relations – a report by the Berlin Correspondent of *The Times*, 1897
The scheme is most important. To my mind it means that for years to come the agitation against England here will be conducted in an intensified form ... it would give the 'nation' a cause to spout about and since 1870 and more especially since 1888 the Government cannot get on without excitement ... Else the electors would begin to propose reforms, to tinker with the constitution, assail the privileges of the Army and other classes.

From Paul Kennedy: *The Rise of Anglo-German Antagonism 1860–1914* (1982)

V   Joseph Chamberlain's proposals for better relations, a confidential Memorandum by Bülow, visiting England, 24 November 1899
His Majesty the Emperor honoured Mr Chamberlain after the banquet of the 21st with a long conversation. In answer to the Colonial Secretary's remark that he desired a general understanding between Germany, England and America His Majesty said that a general *rapprochement* of this sort had objections for both sides. Whilst it was not in the British tradition to conclude formal alliances, definite political frontiers were drawn for Germany for some time to come by her excellent relations with Russia. But there were several points on which Germany and England might agree as they turned up. Both countries ought to follow up the method of special agreements which had been tried with success on two occasions. His Majesty added that it was to England's interest to handle carefully the sensitive, obstinate and rather sentimental German and not to make him impatient, but to show him good-will in small

matters. The German was 'touchy'; the more this was borne in mind by the British the better for the relations between the two countries.

On November 22nd Mr Balfour visited me. He said that here all parties wished for a *rapprochement* with us and, if possible, also with America at the same time. I answered that our wishes regarding England were more negative than positive. We had no positive requests to make of England nor any positive desires, nor did we make any positive suggestions to England. But we did wish that between England and Germany there should be in future neither misunderstanding nor friction nor needless provocation. Mr Balfour said that no British statesman would fail to subscribe to this programme. In England there was no grudge against Germany's economic development. England was too rich and was herself making too great economic strides to fear German competition to the extent imagined both here and in Germany.

From E.T.S. Dugdale (ed.): *German Diplomatic Documents 1871–1914* (1930)

W Chamberlain's motives, as described by Hartzfeldt reporting to Chancellor Hohenlohe, 2 December 1899

In his speech at Leicester on November 30th, Mr Chamberlain frankly and directly discussed the question of an alliance with Germany. I must refrain for the present from expressing a decided opinion as to his motives on this occasion; so far I can only base it on suppositions, but I intend to return to it later on. But I should like to call attention to the view often expressed to me that Mr Chamberlain is a very shrewd, competent businessman but no diplomat, and that he ties himself down by fixed rules in his dealings. However great may be his personal ambition, I do not consider that it should be assumed that he is entirely guided by it and not by fixed political convictions at the same time. As Your Highness will remember, his idea of an alliance with Germany and America is by no means a new one; a considerable time ago he discussed it with me repeatedly in secret conversations which I reported at the time. His coming out with it now in public proves, in my opinion, that he believes he has most of the Cabinet behind him in that matter, and also that he thinks the moment has come for getting the British public, which so far has been frightened of alliances, used to the idea of one . . .

If I may allow myself an opinion, it can only be useful for us if, without our committing ourselves to any engagement, Mr Chamberlain clings to the hope that we shall end by being persuaded to come in with his wishes for an alliance or a close understanding. At any rate as long as he clings to this hope, he will be accommodating to us in the colonial questions which will probably continue to turn up, and will – as in the

William II's Foreign Policy: The Early Years

Samoa question – try to influence the Cabinet, and especially Lord Salisbury in our favour.
(The Emperor: Correct, and that is the point.)

From E.T.S. Dugdale (ed.): *German Diplomatic Documents 1871–1914* (1930)

X Germany and the Boer War – Bülow's instructions to the German press, 1899

A cool and calm language is recommended for our press towards the English defeat at Ladysmith. A too clearly prominent *Schadenfreude* [spiteful joy] and open jubilation would only turn the bitterness of the English against us, whom we are not yet strong enough to meet at sea, and simultaneously nourish hopes of the French and the Russians that we would be ready to let ourselves be directed alone against England.

From Paul Kennedy: *The Rise of Anglo-German Antagonism 1860–1914* (1982)

Y Holstein writes after the failure of the Anglo-German negotiations for an alliance, 1899–1901

One had the impression that Bülow clung to all the obstacles which stood in the way of the alliance.

From Paul Kennedy: *The Rise of Anglo-German Antagonism 1860–1914* (1982)

Questions

1. How far do Sources A and B substantiate Bismarck's statement in Source C that 'Germany is the single Great Power in Europe which is not tempted by any objects which can only be obtained by a successful war'? **(6 marks)**
2. In Source D what is meant by:
   a 'the Danubian federates of that combination'? **(2 marks)**
   b 'the Mediterranean Agreements of 1887'? **(2 marks)**
3. How far do Sources E and F support the claim made in Source H that Germany should 'lighten Lord Salisbury's task'? **(6 marks)**
4. How far does the map, Source G, illustrate the problem facing Germany in seeking to establish a world role as an imperial power? **(5 marks)**
5. Using your own knowledge and Sources I, J and K, indicate what William II was trying to achieve in his personal contacts with Nicholas II and why he had little chance of being successful. **(8 marks)**
6. In what ways do Sources L and M illustrate the pressures within Germany pushing it towards adoption of 'a more aggressive policy'? **(5 marks)**

9 THE FOREIGN POLICY OF THE GERMAN EMPIRE AND THE OUTBREAK OF WAR IN 1914

Initially German foreign policy in the early 1890s had been based on the conviction that tsarist Russia would not ally itself with revolutionary France. This belief was exposed as mistaken when the Franco-Russian alliance was concluded in 1894, and afterwards considerable, if inconsistent, German efforts were made to draw Russia out of this alliance (see Chapter 8).

Another judgement was that Britain would not be reconciled with France and Russia because of colonial disputes between the powers. However in 1904 Franco-British differences were resolved and the Entente Cordiale (commitment to friendship) was concluded – another setback for German policy. Germany then made efforts to drive Britain and France apart, while at the same time seeking to resolve German differences with the British government [A].

In 1904 the French government, exploiting its agreement with Britain, began to expand its influence in Morocco [B, C]. In response William II, who was on a Mediterranean cruise, was persuaded by Holstein and Bülow to visit Tangier where he promised the Sultan of Morocco that German support would be provided to maintain Moroccan independence. It was anticipated in this way that France would be humiliated and that the Anglo-French Entente would be destroyed. France seemed to confirm German hopes when she agreed that the Moroccan question should be resolved by an international conference at Algeçiras in 1906 [D, E]. The result of the Algeçiras Conference was certainly not what Germany had anticipated [F]. Britain was alarmed that Germany might acquire a base on the Moroccan coast to threaten Gibraltar and, as a result, was driven closer to France [G] while identifying German policy as dangerous [H].

In the meantime, faced with the possibility of a war on two fronts against France and Russia, the Chief of the German general staff, Alfred von Schlieffen, devised a war plan to achieve German victory. This involved, in the event of war, the immediate invasion of France and her defeat within forty days, with the invading German army advancing through Belgium and Holland [I, J].

After the disappointment of 1906, Germany continued to increase the size of its navy [K], even though this was bound to worsen relations with Britain [L]. In fact the German government felt that its international

The Foreign Policy of the German Empire and the Outbreak of War in 1914

position was weakened when the British government resolved its outstanding disputes with Russia in 1907 and the Entente Cordiale between France and Britain became the Triple Entente with the inclusion of Russia. However, this was not the end of German attempts to improve Anglo-German relations [M, N], but Britain was suspicious of the continuing growth of the German navy and more interested in preserving the Triple Entente.

In 1908 a dangerous crisis occurred in the Balkans. Austria–Hungary, alarmed by a possible revival of the Ottoman Empire, annexed Bosnia and Herzegovina, the Turkish provinces she had occupied since 1878. This action annoyed the Serbian government and represented a diplomatic defeat for Russia, the champion of Serb interests. Germany gave total backing to the Austrian government [O, P].

In 1911 Germany provoked a second Moroccan crisis. A French expeditionary force was sent to Fez to assist the Sultan, thereby infringing the Algeçiras agreement [Q]. In retaliation the German gunboat *Panther* anchored off the port of Agadir with the intention of staying there until Germany received compensation for the French action [R]. Britain again reacted strongly by backing France [S]; in particular a speech by Lloyd George, the Chancellor of the Exchequer, emphasised the British position [T]. In the outcome Germany acquired a largely worthless tract of land in Central Africa at the expense of antagonising the Entente powers. But a further attempt to improve Anglo-German relations was made by Lord Haldane, the British Minister for War, who visited Berlin in 1912 [U]. However, Germany was not prepared to limit her naval building programme and the negotiations failed.

The European powers were able to resolve the problems produced by the two Balkan wars of 1912 and 1913 against Turkey but the end result was a doubling in the size and power of Serbia. Any increase in Serbian strength was identified as a threat by the Austro-Hungarian government. At the end of 1913 Russo-German relations were strained by the appointment of a German general, Liman von Sanders, to command the Constantinople garrison [V].

The Balkans were thus the potential flashpoint for Europe. This became actuality when Archduke Ferdinand, the heir to the Austrian throne, was assassinated in Sarajevo at the end of June 1914. The Austrian government saw this as the opportunity to crush the Serbs. Germany gave unconditional backing to its Austrian allies [W], even though this risked war with Russia [X]. After a delay Austria issued an ultimatum to Serbia and followed this with a declaration of war in spite of Russian mobilisation [Y]. This in turn produced German mobilisation.

Excluding the invasion of Holland, the German general staff insisted on implementing the Schlieffen Plan. An ultimatum was issued to France and Belgium, followed by the invasion of both countries on 3 August 1914.

After the war many historians attributed its outbreak to the failure of diplomatic relations between the powers, a failure for which all the participants were equally to blame. However, since the 1960s historians like Fritz Fischer have claimed that the German government deliberately precipitated war in 1914, in response to domestic social and political pressures [Z]. As a result attention has increasingly been turned to the political and social pressures throughout Europe to find an explanation for the start of the 1914–18 war.

A Holstein, writing in 1905, recognises the need to improve Anglo–German relations

The place where German policy should dig in is in England not France ... We should use the next few years, when Russia will be occupied by her own affairs, to prevent England from joining the Dual Alliance. Without England, even the Dual Alliance will think twice before making war on us.

From Paul Kennedy: *The Rise of Anglo-German Antagonism 1860–1914* (1982)

B Baron von Mentingen, the Minister at Tangier, writing to Bülow in April 1904 justifies German involvement in Morocco

At this moment when the war in the Far East and the revolt in [German] South-West Africa are attracting universal attention, I think that German action in Morocco ought to be even further from our thoughts than before. Nevertheless, in consideration of the demand of the Morocco Company, in its recent memorial to Your Excellency, for compensation for a certain strengthening of France's position in Morocco, I think it should be pointed out that the Moorish Government's slackness after Dr Genthe's murder [the Correspondent of the *Kolnische Zeitung*], and its illegal action in the case of Ben Zakur give us such a motive for forcible intervention as may not occur again. Moreover, so long as France has not advanced further than at present in extending her influence in Morocco, she would feel less mortified now, supposing we occupied a point on the coast – say, Agadir and its neighbourhood – than later on, when she will have consolidated her domination. The Imperial Admiralty may already have decided on the method of realising such action. I would merely remark humbly that, in addition to the ships engaged in the operation, one warship should be stationed at Tangier to protect Europeans, and another should be cruising along the coast. Also the Germans at Marakesh should be summoned away in good time.

From E.T.S. Dugdale (ed.): *German Diplomatic Documents 1871–1914* (1930)

The Foreign Policy of the German Empire and the Outbreak of War in 1914

C Bülow's interpretation of the Moroccan question

French Moroccan policy was an obvious attempt to set Germany aside in an important decision on foreign affairs, an attempt to adjust the balance of power in Europe in favour of France. A precedent would have been established which must of necessity have tempted to repetition. We could not risk that. From this point of view the Moroccan affair became a national question for us. The course of our policy in Morocco was clearly indicated.

From Bernhard von Bülow: *Imperial Germany* (1914)

D Chancellor Bülow writes in September 1905 of the Moroccan crisis

All that matters is for us to find a way out of this Moroccan business so as to keep our prestige in the world intact, while taking account as far as possible of German economic and financial interests.

From Alan Palmer: *The Kaiser* (1978)

E Enthusiasm for the Algeçiras Conference
(i) Holstein's view
It is most unlikely that a conference will give Morocco to France against the vote of Germany and America.
(ii) Chancellor Bülow's opinion
It is out of the question that the conference will result in a majority handing over Morocco to France.

From A.J.P. Taylor: *The Struggle for Mastery in Europe 1848–1914* (1954)

F The British attitude at the Algeçiras Conference as conveyed to Bülow by Count von Metternich, visiting London in January 1906

Today I had an important conversation about Morocco with Sir Edward Grey [Foreign Secretary 1905–16]. Since my recent conversation with him I have been careful not to mention it to him; but today he began upon it himself.

I will first say that Sir Edward Grey gives me the impression of being a frank, straightforward man, and that one knows where one is with him.

He said that the approaching Morocco Conference filled him with anxiety; to which I replied that I could not escape the same feeling. Since our last meeting he had further examined the Morocco question, which was his reason for referring to it again with me. The Entente with France and the removal of the old quarrels were very greatly welcomed in England, and they wished to keep to it and run no risks with it. The feeling was general here that England must not leave the French

Confederation to Empire

Government in the lurch in a question arising out of the Anglo-French Agreement. This was the standpoint of the British Government, whether Liberal or Conservative. He thought it right to tell me his views frankly before the Conference met, for differences might arise at it between Germany and France which would make it harder for him, as a British Minister to discuss it.

From E.T.S. Dugdale (ed.): *German Diplomatic Documents 1871–1914* (1930)

G William II, in exile in Holland in 1930, considers Algeçiras in retrospect

Algeçiras was the outcome of the totally wrong policy of Holstein–Bülow which forced me to go to Tangier. The curse of constitutionalism. Had I not been a constitutional monarch, tied to my advisers by a constitution, but been free to govern like Frederick the Great then the visit to Tangier would never have taken place and neither would Algeçiras. France would have reached an arrangement suitable to herself. Bülow pursued prestige politics which, though abhorrent to me, everywhere aroused suspicion that I had ordered him to do so, whereas he could hide behind me if they should fail – 'The Kaiser must be made to look ridiculous or be humiliated': a consequence of the advantageous position enjoyed by the chancellor over the Kaiser.

From Alan Palmer: *The Kaiser* (1978)

H The British view of German aims as expressed in 1907 by Sir Eyre Crowe, a senior British Foreign Office official

Germany had won her place as one of the leading, if not, in fact, the foremost power on the European continent. But over and beyond the European great powers there seemed to stand the 'world powers'. It was at once clear that Germany must become a 'world power'. The evolution of this idea and its translation into practical politics followed with singular consistency the line of thought that had inspired the Prussian kings in their efforts to make Prussia great. 'If Prussia,' said Frederick the Great, 'is to count for something in the councils of Europe, she must be made a great power.' And the echo: 'If Germany wants to have a voice in the affairs of the larger oceanic world she must be made a ''world power''.' 'I want more territory,' said Prussia. 'Germany must have colonies,' says the new world-policy. And colonies were accordingly established, in such spots as were found to be still unappropriated, or out of which others could be pushed by the vigorous assertion of a German demand for 'a place in the sun'. On the whole, however, the 'Colonies' have proved assets of somewhat doubtful value.

The Foreign Policy of the German Empire and the Outbreak of War in 1914

Meanwhile the dream of a colonial empire had taken deep hold on the German imagination. Emperor, statesmen, journalists, geographers, economists, commercial and shipping houses and the whole mass of educated and uneducated public opinion continue with one voice to declare: We *must* have real colonies, where German emigrants can settle and spread the national ideals of the Fatherland and we *must* have a fleet and coaling stations to keep together the colonies which we are bound to acquire ...

From J.C.G. Roehl (ed.): *From Bismarck to Hitler* (1970)

I A later description of the disadvantages of the Schlieffen Plan
The most severe charge against Schlieffen, Moltke and the general staff is that they formulated a purely military plan which ignored the political dimension. Schlieffen certainly gave military needs complete priority: if France were to be defeated in six weeks, armies of a certain size were necessary; if they could only find the room to deploy by passing through neutral Holland and Belgium, so be it. Schlieffen was aware that this blatant violation of neutral states was to bring Britain into the war, but calculated that her forces would be too late and too small to save France from defeat. What remains truly astonishing was that Schlieffen formulated and retained a plan without alternatives which committed Germany to an immediate all-out attack on France no matter when or how the war began.

From Brian Bond: *War and Society in Europe 1870–1970* (1984)

J Holstein, commenting in 1897 on the significance of the supremacy of military leaders in Germany
If the head of the great General Staff, and especially a strategic authority like Schlieffen, considers such a measure (the violating of Belgium and Luxemburg) essential, then it is the duty of diplomacy to adjust itself accordingly and to prepare for it in all possible ways.

From Brian Bond: *War and Society in Europe 1870–1970* (1984)

Confederation to Empire

K The military strength of the world powers in 1906
(i) Chief armies of the world

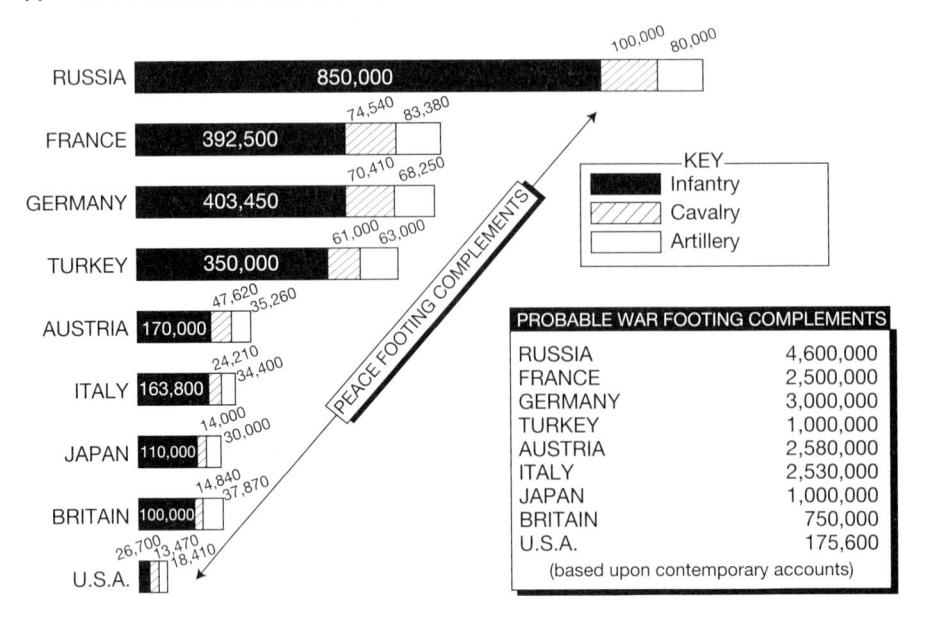

Chief armies of the world (Infantry / Cavalry / Artillery):

- RUSSIA: 850,000 / 100,000 / 80,000
- FRANCE: 392,500 / 74,540 / 83,380
- GERMANY: 403,450 / 70,410 / 68,250
- TURKEY: 350,000 / 61,000 / 63,000
- AUSTRIA: 170,000 / 47,620 / 35,260
- ITALY: 163,800 / 24,210 / 34,400
- JAPAN: 110,000 / 14,000 / 30,000
- BRITAIN: 100,000 / 14,840 / 37,870
- U.S.A.: 26,700 / 13,470 / 18,410

(PEACE FOOTING COMPLEMENTS)

KEY:
- Infantry
- Cavalry
- Artillery

PROBABLE WAR FOOTING COMPLEMENTS	
RUSSIA	4,600,000
FRANCE	2,500,000
GERMANY	3,000,000
TURKEY	1,000,000
AUSTRIA	2,580,000
ITALY	2,530,000
JAPAN	1,000,000
BRITAIN	750,000
U.S.A.	175,600

(based upon contemporary accounts)

(ii) Chief navies of the world (1906 was the year the British 'Dreadnought' battleship was launched)

COUNTRY	BATTLESHIPS (first class)	BATTLESHIPS (other classes)	CRUISERS (first class)	CRUISERS (other classes)	DESTROYERS, SUBMARINES, M.T.B.s	OFFICERS & MEN
BRITAIN	45	15	38	87	232	129,000
U.S.A.	15	11	7	14	47	37,000
FRANCE	11	19	10	37	271	29,500
GERMANY	18	13	6	24	103	33,500
RUSSIA	4	7	2	10	145	60,000
ITALY	4	9	3	17	61	26,800
JAPAN	10	4	9	17	72	36,000

Note: it was the axiom of British naval policy that her navy should roughly equal in strength the combined fleets of the next two largest naval powers.

The Foreign Policy of the German Empire and the Outbreak of War in 1914

L The problems of increasing the pace of German battleship building summarised by Dahnärt, adviser to Tirpitz, in February 1907
Should Germany introduce a temporary building tempo of four ships per annum over the next few years and for no recognisable reason, the stigma of having caused a fruitless arms race will be impressed on us and the German Empire will encounter even greater animosities than at present when our reputation as a troublemaker is bad enough ... The Liberal Cabinet in Britain will be thrown out of office and be replaced by a Conservative one, which, even if one hopes for the best, will, by making huge investments in the Navy, completely obliterate all our chances of catching up with Britain's maritime power within a measurable space of time.

From V.R. Berghahn: *Germany and the Approach of War in 1914* (1973)

M The reaction of the British press to the expansion of the German navy, relayed to Bülow on 14 December 1907 by Count Metternich, the German Ambassador in London
There are again today some articles in the British Press on the German Naval Programme. Yesterday the *Westminster Gazette* published a letter from the President of the Navy League [R.A. Yerburgh] referring to the coming increase of the German fleet and warning the British Government to maintain the British fleet in sufficient strength to be able to destroy any foreign coalition at sea. It should be done as in 1898, when the British Government, on learning of the increase of the Russian fleet, at once increased the programme of the year by four battleships and four armoured cruisers. This measure kept within its own hearth the fire which soon afterwards broke out in the Far East.

The *Daily Graphic* today fully agrees with this expression of opinion by the Navy League and asks why Germany considers this enormous increase necessary just when strong efforts are being made to produce friendly relations between England and Germany. (The Emperor: 'Navy Bill published 10 years ago.') England must observe this and act accordingly. Whatever the expense of assuring England's position on the sea England must and will see to it.

From E.T.S. Dugdale (ed.): *German Diplomatic Documents 1871–1914* (1930)

N William II, writing in English to the British First Lord of the Admiralty in February 1908, makes an unusual attempt to reassure British opinion about German warship building
It is absolutely nonsensical and untrue that the German Navy Bill is to provide a Navy meant 'as a challenge to British naval supremacy'. The

Confederation to Empire

German fleet is built against nobody at all. It is solely built for Germany's needs in relation with that country's rapidly growing trade.

From V.R. Berghahn: *Germany and the Approach of War in 1914* (1973)

O   William II writes to Archduke Ferdinand in December 1908 on the Austrian annexation of Bosnia–Herzegovina
I hold myself prepared for everything that God may ordain. I keep my powder dry and am on my guard. You know that you may count on us.

From Alan Palmer: *The Kaiser* (1978)

P   The Chancellor's reaction to the annexation
Our position would indeed be dangerous if Austria lost confidence and turned away. So long as we stand together, we form a bloc that no one will lightly attack. In eastern questions above all, we cannot place ourselves in opposition to Austria who has nearer and greater interests in the Balkan peninsula than ourselves. A refusal or a grudging attitude in the question of annexation of Bosnia and Herzegovina would not be forgiven.

From Gordon Craig: *Germany 1866–1945* (1978)

Q   William II's view on the situation in Morocco, expressed to Chancellor Bethmann-Hollweg in April 1911
If the French break the Algeçiras Agreement, we can leave it to the other powers, and especially Spain, to protest first. We can do nothing with warships... I therefore beg you to stand firm against sending warships.

From Alan Palmer: *The Kaiser* (1978)

R   The German Foreign Office view, expressed in a memorandum dated 3 May 1911 by Alfred von Kiderlen-Wachter, Foreign Minister
The occupation of Fez would pave the way for the absorption of Morocco by France. We should gain nothing by protesting and it would mean a moral defeat hard to bear. We must therefore look for an objective for the ensuing negotiations, which shall induce the French to compensate us. If the French out of 'anxiety' for their compatriots, settle themselves at Fez, it is our right, too, to protect our compatriots in danger. We have large German firms at Mogador and Agadir. German ships could go to those ports to protect the firms. They could remain anchored there quite peacefully – merely with the idea of preventing other Powers from intruding into these very important harbours of southern Morocco. The importance of choosing these ports, the great distance of which from the Mediterranean should make it unlikely that England would raise objections, lies in the fact that they possess a very

fertile hinterland, which ought to contain important mineral wealth as well. The Hamburg firm of Warburg & Co., for instance, have recently been able to prove considerable deposits of copper. Moreover the powerful Kaids of the district have been for many years friendly with the German firm of Weiss & Mauer at Mogador, so that by skilful handling of the affair it might be possible to prevent any unrest in the hinterland of the two ports. Regarding Agadir I may remark that it is long since it has counted as one of the 'open ports' of Morocco, but it is one of the best harbours on the Atlantic coast of that country.

In possession of such a pledge we should look confidently on at the further development of affairs in Morocco and see whether France will offer us proper compensation in her own colonial possessions, in return for which we could abandon the two ports.

From E.T.S. Dugdale (ed.): *German Diplomatic Documents 1871–1914* (1930)

S   The British view of the second Moroccan crisis summarised by Sir Eyre Crowe in July 1911

Germany is playing for the highest stakes. If her demands are acceded to either on the Congo or in Morocco – what she will, I believe, try for – in both regions, it will mean definitely the subjugation of France. The conditions demanded are not such as a country having an independent foreign policy can possibly accept. The details of the terms are not so very important now. It is a trial of strength, if anything. Concession means not loss of interest or loss of prestige, it means defeat with all its inevitable consequences.

From V.R. Berghahn: *Germany and the Approach of War in 1914* (1973)

T   The German reaction to Lloyd George's speech, contained in a letter from Kiderlen-Wachter to the German Ambassador in London, 24 July 1911

The text of the Chancellor of the Exchequer's recent speech, which has just come to hand, has caused most of the British and all the French papers to attack Germany violently. I do not suggest how far this result was intended by the British Minister. But the British Government will be unable to prevent the impression being that this effect of a speech by one of their number is bound to cause great annoyance here, especially since this effect, combined with Sir E. Grey's statements to Your Excellency, might appear to us not wholly unintentional.

Nevertheless if England felt bound to express any wishes, we could wait for them to be communicated to us through the usual diplomatic channels. But if, instead of this, the British Government allowed one of their members to make a public declaration which might be construed at the least as a warning addressed to us, and was in fact construed by

British and French papers as a warning bordering on a threat, we find it hard to admit the grounds for this. The British Government could not have been unaware that this would not help on a friendly understanding between us and France, which they themselves assert that they desire. Considering the hostile tone adopted by some of the British and all the French papers for some time past the British Government must have realised the result to be expected from the speech of the Chancellor of the Exchequer.

If it was the British Government's intention to complicate and confuse the political situation and bring about a settlement by means of force, they could not have chosen a better way than by the Chancellor's speech, which so ignored the dignity which he claimed for England or the position of a Great Power such as ourselves.

From E.T.S. Dugdale (ed.): *German Diplomatic Documents 1871–1914* (1930)

U   British terms for improved Anglo-German relations, communicated to Chancellor Bethmann-Hollweg by the British banker Sir Ernest Cassel in January 1912
1   Fundamental. Naval superiority recognised as essential to Great Britain. Present German naval programme and expenditure not to be increased, but if possible retarded and reduced.
2   England sincerely desires not to interfere with German colonial expansion. To give effect to this she is prepared forthwith to discuss whatever the German aspirations in this direction may be. England will be glad to know that there is a field or special points where she can help Germany.
3   Proposals for reciprocal assurances debarring either power from joining in aggressive designs or combinations against the other would be welcome.

From V.R. Berghahn: *Germany and the Approach of War in 1914* (1973)

V   The disturbing impact of Liman von Sanders as head of the German Military Mission to the Ottoman Empire
(i)   Sazanov, Russian Foreign Minister, to a German journalist, 1913
You know what interests we have at the Bosphorus, how sensitive we are at that point. All Southern Russia depends on it and now you stick a Prussian garrison under our noses.
(ii)   Tsar Nicholas II, December 1913
To abandon the straits to a powerful state would be synonymous with subordinating the whole economic development of Southern Russia to that state.

From V.R. Berghahn: *Germany and the Approach of War in 1914* (1973)

The Foreign Policy of the German Empire and the Outbreak of War in 1914

W Germany's guarantee of unconditional support to Austria, conveyed by the Austrian Ambassador in Berlin to the Austrian Foreign Minister in July 1914
Strictly Confidential
The Kaiser authorised me to inform our gracious majesty that we might in this case, as in all others, rely upon Germany's full support ... he did not doubt in the least that Herr von Bethmann-Hollweg would agree with him. Especially as far as our action against Serbia was concerned. But it was his [Kaiser Wilhelm's] opinion that this action must not be delayed. Russia's attitude will no doubt be hostile, but for this he had for years prepared, and should a war between Austria–Hungary and Russia be unavoidable, we might be convinced that Germany, our old faithful ally, would stand at our side. Russia at the present time was in no way prepared for war, and would think twice before it appealed to arms ... if we had really recognised the necessity of warlike action against Serbia, he (Kaiser Wilhelm) would regret if we did not make use of the present moment, which is all in our favour ...

From I. Geiss: *July 1914 – Selected Documents* (1967)

X Moltke's view of the German military position, recorded by the State Secretary, the German Foreign Office, May 1914
The prospects of the future seriously worried him. Russia will have completed her armaments in two to three years. The military superiority of our enemies would be so great that he did not know how to cope with them. In his view there was no alternative to waging a preventive war in order to defeat the enemy as long as we could still more or less pass the test. The Chief of the General Staff left it to my discretion to gear our policy to an early unleashing of a war.

From V.R. Berghahn: *Germany and the Approach of War in 1914* (1973)

Y William II attempts to halt Russian mobilisation in an exchange of telegrams with Nicholas II
(i) William II to Nicholas II on 29 July 1914
I received your telegram and share your wish that peace should be maintained. But as I told you in my first telegram, I cannot consider Austria's action against Serbia an 'ignoble' war. Austria knows by experience that Serbian promises on paper are wholly unreliable. I understand its action must be judged as tending to get full guarantee that the Serbian promises shall become real facts. Thus my reasoning is borne out by the statement of the Austrian Cabinet that Austria does not want to make any territorial conquests at the expense of Serbia. I therefore suggest that it would be quite possible for Russia to remain a spectator of the Austro-Serbian conflict without involving Europe in the

most horrible war she ever witnessed. I think a direct understanding between your Government and Vienna possible and desirable and as I already telegraphed to you my Government is continuing its exertions to promote it. Of course military measures on the part of Russia which would be looked on by Austria as threatening would precipitate a calamity we both wish to avoid and jeopardise my position as mediator which I readily accepted on your appeal to my friendship and my help.

(ii) Nicholas II to William II on 30 July 1914

Thank you heartily for your quick answer. Am sending Tatistchev [the Russian officer attending William II] this evening with instructions. The *military measures which have now come into force were decided five days ago* for reasons of *defence on account of Austria's preparations*. I hope from all my heart that these measures *won't in any way interfere* with your part as mediator which I greatly value. *We need your strong pressure on Austria* to come to an *understanding with us.*

(iii) William's comments on the telegram of 30 July 1914

No! There is no thought of anything of that sort!!! Austria has only made a *partial* mobilisation against *Serbia* in the *south*. On the strength of that the Tsar – as is openly admitted by him here – instituted 'mil. measures which have now *come into force*' against Austria and us and as a matter of fact five days ago. Thus it is almost a *week ahead* of us. And these measures are for *defence* against *Austria*, which is in no way attacking him!!! I cannot agree to any more mediation, since the Tsar who requested it has at the same time secretly mobilised behind my back. It is only a manoeuvre, in order to hold us back and to increase the start they have already got. My work is at an end!

From I. Geiss: *July 1914 – Selected Documents* (1967)

Z The Russian Ambassador in Berlin in 1909 warns about German militarism

The war party, tempted by the unquestionable military preparedness of the army and the other classes of society, hurt in its feelings of traditional loyalty to the Supreme Commander regards war as the only possible means of restoring, in the eyes of the masses, the monarchy's shaken prestige.

Feeling in military circles is moving towards the conviction that the superiority of the army at the present moment promises the greatest prospects of success for Germany. Such a conviction might tempt this Emperor and give his foreign policy a militant character.

Moreover, a victorious war could, at least at first, reduce the pressure of the radical movement in the people for a change of both the Prussian and the Imperial constitution on more liberal lines. These – in general

The Foreign Policy of the German Empire and the Outbreak of War in 1914

terms – are the symptoms of domestic life in Germany which can explain the reasons for military preparations.

From Gordon Craig: *Germany 1866–1945* (1978)

Questions

1. In Source A, Holstein in 1905 argues that the 'next few years should be used to prevent England from joining the Dual Alliance'. What light do Sources L to O shed on the pursuit of this policy? **(10 marks)**
2. How far do Sources B to G and your own knowledge support William II's statement that Algeçiras was 'the outcome of a totally wrong policy'? **(10 marks)**
3. Does Source H sustain Eyre Crowe's argument that the *Weltpolitik* of Imperial Germany follows 'with singular consistency the line of thought that had inspired Prussian kings'? **(5 marks)**
4. What evidence is there in Sources I and J regarding the degree of influence exerted by the military leaders in William II's Germany? **(6 marks)**
5. Does Source K bear out Germany's fears of 'encirclement' in the years preceding 1914? **(4 marks)**
6. Drawing on your own knowledge and the evidence of Sources O and P, examine the view that the German backing for Austria in 1908 was a mistaken policy. **(6 marks)**
7. How far do Sources R to T justify the view expressed by William II in Source Q that Germany should send no warships to the Moroccan coast? **(8 marks)**
8. How far does Source U substantiate the view that Haldane's Mission to Berlin in 1912 had no chance of success? **(5 marks)**
9. What evidence is there in Sources V to Z for the statement that 'Germany's past record was not one to arouse much confidence in its ability to pursue foreign policy calmly and rationally'? **(10 marks)**

10 THE GERMANY OF BISMARCK AND WILLIAM II: A HISTORICAL PERSPECTIVE

For many commentators Bismarck was the man who created the German Empire. However, his role has been questioned by some modern historians who have also identified underlying weaknesses in his creation. In addition there has been considerable debate about the causes of the 1914–18 war. How far was this the product of Bismarck's *Reich*, how far the product of William II's governments? The debate continues but most historians now agree that the actions of Germany contributed more to the outbreak of war in 1914 than those of any other power.

A William Carr, a specialist on modern German history, attributes to Bismarck a crucial weakness in being essentially a man of the eighteenth century

Like all great men he had serious defects and limitations. He was petty, vindictive and ruthless in his treatment of those who stood in his way. His tyrannical methods, intolerance of independence of mind in others and his lust for power left their mark on the whole apparatus of government, infecting subordinates with the corruption of manners inevitable in a personal dictatorship. His most serious limitation was that he was cast in the mould of the eighteenth century. To him government was essentially a function of rulers and officials, not peoples. Most certainly he had some understanding of the dynamic political and social implications of an industrial society. But his Bonapartist methods – seeking to satisfy the material interests of aristocracy, middle class and (to some extent) working class while barring the way to more responsible government – seriously retarded Germany's political growth.

From William Carr: *A History of Germany 1815–1990* (1991)

B Alan Palmer, a recent biographer of Bismarck, while acknowledging his statesmanship, blames him for many of the problems of the German Empire between 1870 and 1914

Though Bismarck became, belatedly, a hero symbol of conservative resistance to Nazism, it is not possible to exonerate him entirely from responsibility for the rapid growth of diplomatic anarchy in the twentieth century. His manipulation of the press, his ingenious resort to

The Germany of Bismarck and William II: A Historical Perspective

stratagems which ran counter to his commitments, his use of half-truths, bombast and intimidation – all these aspects of his system were to become commonplace at a time when foreign policy was being shaped by lesser men who lacked his resourcefulness in avoiding war. The supreme quality of Bismarck's statesmanship was his recognition that no policy could be pursued beyond a certain danger limit, and that it was essential to have alternatives ready for dignified retreat and redeployment. Few politicians in Germany, or in other lands, have possessed such suppleness of mind.

From Alan Palmer: *Bismarck* (1976)

C   Hans-Ulrich Wehler, a prominent German historian, emphasises the problems of the German Empire created by Bismarck, summarising his regime as being in many ways a 'Bonapartist' dictatorship
Bismarck's greater Prussian Imperial state, as founded in 1871, was the product of the 'revolution from above' in its military stage. The legitimacy of the young *Reich* had no generally accepted basis, nor was it founded upon a generally accepted code of basic political convictions, as was to be immediately demonstrated in the years of crisis after 1873. Bismarck had to cover up the social and political differences in the tension-ridden class society of his new Germany, and to this end he relied on a technique of negative integration. His method was to inflame the conflicts between those groups which were allegedly hostile to the *Reich*, *Reichsfeinde*, like the Socialists and Catholics, left-wing liberals and Jews on the one hand, and those groups which were allegedly loyal to the *Reich*, the *Reichsfreunde*. It was thanks to the permanent conflict between these in-and-out groups that he was able to achieve variously composed majorities for his policies. The Chancellor was thus under constant pressure to provide rallying points for his *Reichspolitik*, and so to legitimise his system by periodically producing fresh political successes. Within a typology of contemporary power structures in the second half of the nineteenth century Bismarck's régime can be classified as a Bonapartist dictatorship: a traditional unstable social and political structure which found itself threatened by strong forces of social and political change, which was to be defended and stabilised by diverting attention away from constitutional policy towards economic policy, away from questions of emancipation at home towards compensatory successes abroad; these ends were to be further achieved by undisguised repression as well as by limited concessions. In this way also the neo-absolutist pseudo-constitutional dictatorship of the Chancellor could be maintained. By guaranteeing the bourgeoisie protection from the workers' demands for political and social emancipation in exchange for its own political abdication, the dictatorial

executive gained a noteworthy degree of political independence vis-à-vis the component social groups and economic interests. And just as overseas expansion, motivated by domestic and economic considerations, had become an element of the political style of French Bonapartism, so Bismarck too, after a short period of consolidation in foreign affairs, saw the advantages of such expansion as an antidote to recurring economic setbacks and to the permanent direct or latent threat to the whole system and became the 'Caesarist statesman'.

From Hans-Ulrich Wehler: *The German Empire 1870–1918* (1985)

D V.R. Berghahn, a German historian who has written extensively on German politics before 1914, identifies the German problem as that of a country industrialising rapidly but with a political system unable to cope with the change

The pre-1914 period has often been described as the 'golden age' of Europe. By comparison with what followed after 1914 this may well be true. But such comparisons can easily mislead one into thinking that it was all peace and prosperity. It is probably more accurate to say that behind a splendid façade there existed an international community convulsed by growing conflict. The metaphor is certainly applicable to the Wilhelmine Empire which in the second half of the nineteenth century had undergone a particularly rapid process of industrialisation. This process, it is true, had led to the creation of new wealth and unprecedented prosperity. But what made the splendour so deceptive was that technological and economic changes took place in a country whose social and political structures were poorly prepared for industrialisation. These structures had been established in the pre-industrial era and continued to be controlled by an élite whose economic power base was agriculture and whose existence was threatened by the factory. Not surprisingly, perhaps, the agrarians continued to use their key position within the political system to contain this threat and to secure their survival. To put it differently: those groups in German society which were most strategically placed to initiate structural reforms were opposed to any kind of social and political modernisation and, with the passage of time, actually came to resist it with increasing vigour. In their view there was only one solution to the problems raised by industrialisation of the country, namely to preserve at all cost the existing distribution of power within state and society. There was no other way, they believed, of maintaining their privileges and providing them with such subsidies as were deemed necessary to prevent their economic decline.

From V.R. Berghahn: *Germany and the Approach of War in 1914* (1973)

E Fritz Fischer is the German historian who identified German policies as being the prime cause of the outbreak of war in 1914. Here he states that Germany faced major economic problems before the outbreak of war

Germany's claim to world power was based on her consciousness of being a 'young', growing and rising nation. Her population had risen from about 41 millions in 1871 to about 68 millions in 1915, while that of France, with a larger area, had remained almost stationary, reaching only 40 millions in 1915. Moreover, more than one-third of the population of Germany was under 15 years of age, and this gave the national consciousness a dynamic element which further reinforced the demand for *Lebensraum* [living space], markets and industrial expansion. Although emigration had been high (1.3 million persons emigrated between 1881 and 1890), the population figures for 1910 were nevertheless far more favourable than, for example, those of France: an excess of births over deaths of 800 000 (8.9 per thousand against 3.4 per thousand in France), while the expectation of life was increasing and infant mortality on the decline. With increasing industrialisation, internal migration was beginning to replace migration overseas and immigrants were beginning to come in from Austria, Italy, Russian Poland and other European countries. Germany was developing more and more into a highly industrialised exporting country, and the problem of finding markets and raw materials to support her population was growing increasingly urgent.

From Fritz Fischer: *Germany's Aims in the First World War* (1967)

F Paul Kennedy, who has specialised in the study of diplomatic and naval rivalry, examines the causes of Anglo-German antagonism

Finally, is it possible – and profitable – to grasp the nettle of allocating responsibility for the growth of Anglo-German estrangement and the fact that they eventually fought each other?

There is one quick answer to this question about responsibility, and then a more complicated one. The immediate reply would be that it chiefly rests upon the German side. Had her leaders not been so determined to alter the maritime balance of power after 1897, and to unleash a westward strike in the aftermath of Sarajevo which, with even more certainty, would alter the military balance, then an Anglo-German conflict might well have been avoided. That is, of course, the sort of judgement which the historians and philosophers of Wilhelmine Germany would have felt inappropriate in the arena of power politics. Had not the British themselves conquered a disproportionate share of the globe? Did not Harold Nicolson concede that 'Our own predatory period – and it was disgraceful enough – dated from 1500 to 1900 . . .

Confederation to Empire

Before we blame Germany, we must first blame our own Elizabethans.'? Did not Churchill, even in the midst of the 1913–14 quarrels over the naval estimates, willingly admit: 'We have got all we want in territory, and our claim to be left in unmolested enjoyment of vast and splendid possessions, mainly acquired by violence, largely maintained by force, often seems less reasonable to others than to us.' These are arguments which are still detectable today. 'Was Tirpitz all that much worse than Sir John Fisher?' a recent British reviewer asked. Is it not the case that the Fischer school has refused 'to deal seriously with whether the ambitions [of Imperial Germany] were justified by objective circumstances, by the same general standard of International morality that animated the other powers? ... Was it "wrong" for Germany to want to be a world power like Britain?' Isn't the chorus of denunciations of German policy from Bismarck to Hitler merely a reflection of the disappointment of pro-Western intellectuals, whose 'liberal image' reveals unhistorical wishful thinking?

It is possible, to be sure, to give an Actonian retort to such arguments: namely, that the German desire (and attempt) to grow at the expense of its neighbours cannot be excused by reference to the earlier misdeeds of others, and that it is impossible for the person who knows the post-1914 course of German history not to take an ethical stand. Yet even if one dislikes issuing moral judgements upon the past, there remains the question of whether it was prudent for the German leaders – intent upon improving their country's position – to appeal so often to the code of naked *Machtpolitik* [power politics], to revel in their superior 'realism' and to deprecate the hypocritical liberal concern about means and ends. Whatever the thoughts of Delcassé, Salisbury, Balfour, Grey or Nicholas II, they were not usually to be heard publicly praising 'blood and iron' policies or 'mailed fists'.

From Paul Kennedy: *The Rise of Anglo-German Antagonism 1860–1918* (1982)

The Germany of Bismarck and William II: A Historical Perspective

G In spite of the Triple Alliance the map shows that Austria-Hungary is Germany's only firm ally by 1914

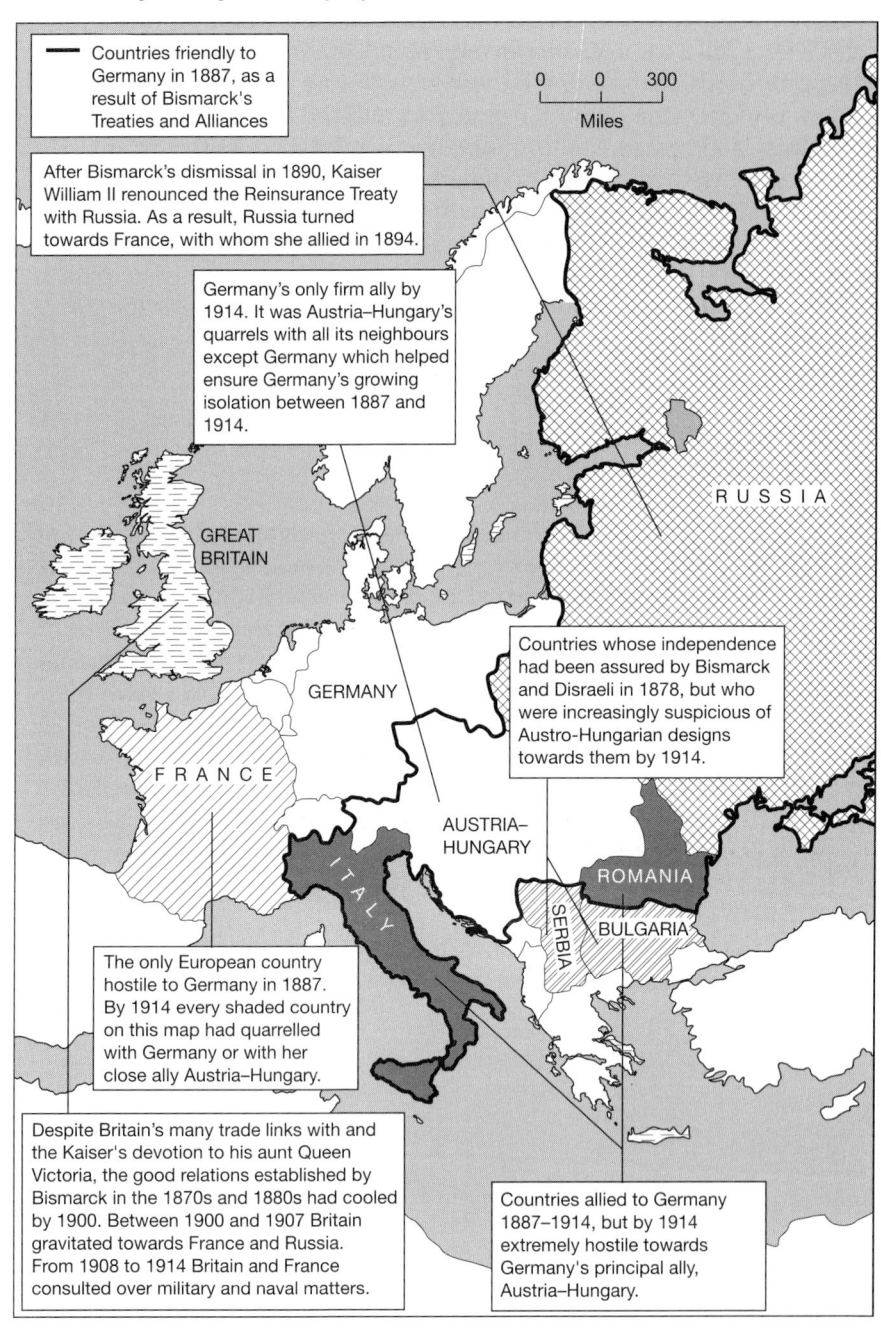

— Countries friendly to Germany in 1887, as a result of Bismarck's Treaties and Alliances

After Bismarck's dismissal in 1890, Kaiser William II renounced the Reinsurance Treaty with Russia. As a result, Russia turned towards France, with whom she allied in 1894.

Germany's only firm ally by 1914. It was Austria–Hungary's quarrels with all its neighbours except Germany which helped ensure Germany's growing isolation between 1887 and 1914.

Countries whose independence had been assured by Bismarck and Disraeli in 1878, but who were increasingly suspicious of Austro-Hungarian designs towards them by 1914.

The only European country hostile to Germany in 1887. By 1914 every shaded country on this map had quarrelled with Germany or with her close ally Austria–Hungary.

Despite Britain's many trade links with and the Kaiser's devotion to his aunt Queen Victoria, the good relations established by Bismarck in the 1870s and 1880s had cooled by 1900. Between 1900 and 1907 Britain gravitated towards France and Russia. From 1908 to 1914 Britain and France consulted over military and naval matters.

Countries allied to Germany 1887–1914, but by 1914 extremely hostile towards Germany's principal ally, Austria–Hungary.

Confederation to Empire

H Immanuel Geiss, who has written on Germany's pre-1914 foreign policy, examines Germany's role in the outbreak of war in July 1914
Two general historical factors proved to be decisive, and both were fused with a third to produce the explosion known as the First World War. Imperialism, with Wilhelmine *Weltpolitik* as its specifically German version, provided the general framework and the basic tensions: the principle of national self-determination constituted, with its revolutionary potential, a permanent but latent threat to the old dynastic Empires and built up tension in South-East Europe. The determination of the German Empire – the most conservative force in the world after Tsarist Russia – to uphold the conservative and monarchic principles, by any means against the rising flood of democracy, plus its *Weltpolitik*, made war inevitable.

From I. Geiss: *July 1914 – Selected Documents* (1967)

Questions

1 What do Sources A and B identify as the strengths and weaknesses of Bismarck? **(7 marks)**
2 In Sources C and D, what are the main problems identified by Hans-Ulrich Wehler and V.R. Berghahn as troubling Imperial Germany before 1914? **(10 marks)**
3 Examine the significance of the following references in Source E:
   a 'more than one third of the population of Germany was under 15 years of age'. **(4 marks)**
   b 'internal migration was beginning to replace migration overseas'. **(4 marks)**
4 In Source F how convincingly does Paul Kennedy establish the case that Germany was more to blame than Britain for the growth of the Anglo-German antagonism? **(10 marks)**
5 In Source H what factors does Immanuel Geiss identify as making the outbreak of war in 1914 inevitable? **(5 marks)**

11 DEALING WITH EXAMINATION QUESTIONS

Specimen Answers to Source-based Questions

Questions based on Chapter 8 – William II's Foreign Policy: The Early Years (see pages 87–99).

Questions

1. How far do Sources A and B substantiate Bismarck's statement in Source C that 'Germany is the single Great Power in Europe which is not tempted by any objects which can only be obtained by a successful war'? **(6 marks)**
2. In Source D what is meant by:
   a 'the Danubian federates of that combination'? **(2 marks)**
   b 'the Mediterranean Agreements of 1887'? **(2 marks)**
3. How far do Sources E and F support the claim made in Source H that Germany should 'lighten Lord Salisbury's task'? **(6 marks)**
4. How far does the map, Source G, illustrate the problem facing Germany in seeking to establish a world role as an imperial power? **(5 marks)**
5. Using your own knowledge and Sources I, J and K, indicate what William II was trying to achieve in his personal contacts with Nicholas II and why he had little chance of being successful. **(8 marks)**
6. In what ways do sources L and M illustrate the pressures within Germany pushing it towards the adoption of a 'more aggressive policy'? **(6 marks)**

Points to Note about these Questions

1. This calls for a careful analysis of what William II and Bernhard von Bülow say about the preservation of peace in Europe. The answer could be solely drawn from the extracts but to give a high quality response to the 'how far' part of the question it is necessary to look at these statements in the context of Germany's international position in the 1890s.
2. The questions about the 'Danubian confederates' of the Triple Alliance and the Mediterranean Agreements of 1887 call on your own knowledge of the background.

Confederation to Empire

  3 The question asks why the granting of Heligoland to Germany was such a difficult concession for Lord Salisbury to make and how far there is evidence that Germany was prepared to make this as easy as possible.
  4 This is a particular style of question asking you to assess visual evidence in the light of your own knowledge.
  5 This question calls for you to examine the reasons stated by William II for improving relations with Tsarist Russia and those given by Nicholas II for ultimately rejecting his overtures. You must use your own knowledge of the background of Russo-German relations to provide a complete answer.
  6 To provide a good answer to this question you must clearly identify the two different sources of pressure arising from Germany's perception of its international position and its intensifying internal problems.

Specimen Answers

  1 How far do Sources A and B substantiate Bismarck's statement in Source C that 'Germany is the single Great Power in Europe which is not tempted by any objects which can only be obtained by a successful war'? **(7 marks)**

William II indicates that he thinks Bismarck's foreign policy has destabilised Europe. He, as the ruler of the country with the most powerful army, will pursue policies to preserve European peace since the other powers will then recognise German superiority. This view is backed by Bernhard von Bülow who states, rather contentiously, that Germany has only fought in the past to defend itself. Now the other powers will be deterred from attacking Germany because of its military power. The weakness of the arguments is that the other European powers were not prepared to concede William II 'a sort of Napoleonic supremacy'. By 1894 the Franco-Russian alliance had been concluded, inspired in part by fear of a German dominated Europe.

  2 In Source D what is meant by:
   a 'the Danubian federates of the combination'? **(2 marks)**

These federates were Serbia and Rumania. In 1881 Austria–Hungary concluded a secret treaty with Serbia and in 1883 Austria–Hungary and Germany both signed an agreement to defend Rumania.

   b 'the Mediterranean Agreements of 1887'? **(2 marks)**

In February 1887 Britain concluded an agreement with Italy and in March with Austria–Hungary to create an arrangement resembling the Triple Entente to preserve the status quo in the Mediterranean region.

Dealing with Examination Questions

3 How far do Sources E and F support the claim made in Source H that Germany should 'lighten Lord Salisbury's task'? **(6 marks)**

The German Chancellor was anxious to keep Salisbury's Conservative government in power since it was identified as being more favourably disposed towards Germany than a Gladstone-led Liberal government. The German foreign office stresses that the importance of Heligoland for Germany should not be emphasised. This will make it easier to arrive at a bargain and also less contentious for Salisbury. Although Hatzfeldt reports that Salisbury is not worried by the reaction of English parliamentary or public opinion Germany is prepared to offer Britain Zanzibar in exchange for this apparently 'valueless' island. The exchange can thus be identified as a triumph for Salisbury.

4 How far does the map, Source G, illustrate the problem facing Germany in seeking to establish a world role as an imperial power?

(5 marks)

Source G shows the three territories in Africa which had become German possessions by 1914 and it also clearly indicates that these can be expanded only at the expense of other European colonial powers. By 1914 only Liberia and Abyssinia remained independent. The limited extent of German territories illustrates that Germany entered the 'scramble for Africa' only belatedly. The map has limitations. It does not tell us that before 1914 Germany had also been ambitious to expand its possessions in Asia and, via the Berlin–Baghdad railway, its influence in the Ottoman Empire.

5 Using your own knowledge and Sources I, J and K, indicate what William II was trying to achieve in his personal contacts with Nicholas II and why he had little chance of being successful. **(8 marks)**

Germany abandoned the Reinsurance Treaty with Russia in 1890 and in 1894 Russia concluded an alliance with France. William, initially through a personal correspondence, is trying to rebuild a Russo-German alliance. To this end he points out that revolutionary republican France is a most unsuitable ally for Tsarist Russia. William points out that it will be advantageous to Russia if Germany safeguards its European interests so that Russian attention can be focused on Asia. At Björkö, Nicholas II's advisers were absent and William thought his efforts had been successful. In the long term there was little chance of this policy succeeding. Germany was allied to Austria–Hungary and Austro-Russian conflicts in the Balkans had already led twice to the collapse of the *Dreikaiserbund*. Moreover, since 1890, Russia had become increasingly dependent on France. France had provided considerable loans which were helping to finance Russian industrialisation.

Confederation to Empire

6 In what ways do Sources L and M illustrate the pressures within Germany pushing it towards the adoption of 'a more aggressive policy'? **(6 marks)**

Admiral von Müller argued in 1896 that Germany, and the other Central European powers, needed overseas possessions as markets for their industrial products and at the same time territories where their surplus population could settle. He stated that achieving this objective was very difficult because of the dominant position in the world held by Britain. The only way to change this was by defeating the British in war. Holstein and Professor Rehm indicated another reason why the German *Reich* needed to fight a successful war; internal discontent was growing so rapidly that the only way of combating it was by establishing Germany as a world power, even if this meant a European war – accepting the danger of 'a world historical gamble'.

Key Points to Note in the Answers

1 Note how this answer combines analysis of the documents with important background material.
2 **a** Only two marks are allocated for this part of the question and the answer identifying Serbia and Rumania is very much to the point.
   b Again precision is called for in this two mark answer, hence the stress upon the formation of a Mediterranean Triple Entente.
3 The answer identifies the difficulties Salisbury might encounter, the motives behind German policy and how these were to be implemented.
4 Observe how the answer demonstrates the problems for Germany in increasing the influence in Africa but also the limitations of the map in demonstrating Germany's world position.
5 A more difficult question: note how the answer uses the evidence in the two documents and a wider knowledge of international relations.
6 Here the answer uses the two sources to illustrate the international and the internal pressures on the German government.

Preparing Essay Answers

Contrary to popular belief, examiners do not enjoy failing candidates. The problems are largely made in the examination room by the candidates themselves. As the reports of the examination boards point out year after year, the greatest single weakness among examinees is an inability to be relevant in their answers. No matter how well read and knowledgeable candidates may be, if they stray too far from the terms of

Dealing with Examination Questions

the question they cannot be given credit. Examinations from A level upwards are basically a test of the candidates' ability to analyse historical material in such a manner as to present a reasoned, informed response to a specific question. Too often examiners are faced with regurgitated notes on a set of topics, little of which relates to the questions as set. There is really no such animal as an 'easy' exam question at these levels; those who set the papers seldom repeat the exact wording of previous questions. This means that each question demands its own individual interpretation. The intelligence and subtlety of the candidates' response will determine how high a mark they score. Examiners must, of course, have 'knowledge', but academic history tests not only *what* they know but how well they *use* what they know. As an aid to the development of effective examination technique, here is a list of questions that candidates should ask themselves when preparing their essays:

1 *Have I answered the question AS SET* or have I simply imposed my prepared answer on it? (It is remarkable how many exam scripts contain answers to questions that do not appear on the exam paper!)

2 *Have I produced a genuine argument* or have I merely put down a number of disconnected points in the hope that the examiners can work it out for themselves? (Too many answers consist of a list of facts rounded off by the 'Thus it can be seen . . .' type of statement which seldom relates to what has been previously written.)

3 *Have I been relevant in arguing my case* or have I included ideas and facts that have no real relation to the question? (Some candidates simply write down all they know about a topic, assuming that sheer volume will overwhelm the examiner into giving a satisfactory mark. This 'mud-at-the-wall' method is counter-productive since it glaringly exposes the candidate's inability to be selective or show judgement.)

4 *Have I made appropriate use of primary or secondary sources to illustrate my answer?* (Examiners do look for evidence of intelligent reading. Choice, apt quotations from documents or books does elevate the quality of an answer. Acquaintance with the ideas of modern historians and authorities is a hallmark of the better prepared candidate. However, discretion needs to be shown; putting in quotations where they are not relevant or inserting over-long, rote-learned passages merely looks like padding.)

5 *Have I tried to show originality* or have I just played safe and written a dully, uninspired answer? (Remember, examiners have to plough through vast quantities of dreary, ill-digested material from large numbers of candidates. When, therefore, they come across a script that shows initiative and zest, their interest and sympathy are engaged.

Candidates who apply their own reasoning and interpretation to questions may occasionally make naive statements but, given that their basic understanding and knowledge are sound, their ambition will be rewarded. This is not an encouragement to 'waffle' but it is to suggest that, provided always that they keep to the terms of the question, candidates are free to follow their own judgements. A thought-provoking answer is likely to be a good answer.)

One final, cautionary, word: never try to be funny in an answer. Humour is like a delicate wine, it does not always travel well. What the candidate thinks is rib-splittingly hilarious may well leave the reader cold. Examiners, like Queen Victoria, are not amused.

Possible Essay Titles

1 How far did the *Zollverein* pave the way for German unification?

Initially the *Zollverein* was intended to create an economically united Prussian state. However, as the majority of German states joined, Prussian leaders like Maasser recognised that Prussian economic leadership could produce Prussian political dominance in the German Confederation. At the beginning the South German liberals opposed the organisation because they thought it would lead to the conquest of South Germany by reactionary Prussia. Before 1848 Metternich recognised the danger that the *Zollverein* would lead to Prussia replacing the Austrian Empire as the dominant German power. In practice by keeping Austria outside the *Zollverein* in the 1850s the position of Prussia as a leading German power was undoubtedly reinforced. At the same time the benefits of the Customs Union contributed to the economic and thus the military development of Prussia. In this way the power base for Bismarck's successes in the 1860s was developed before he became Prussian Chancellor.

2 Why did the Frankfurt Parliament fail in its aims?

The primary aim of the Frankfurt parliamentarians was to establish a united German nation governed by a monarchy with its power limited by an elected assembly. There were a number of factors which contributed to the failure to achieve these objectives. Firstly there was a major disagreement about the frontiers of the German nation – should it be *Grossdeutschland* embracing all German speakers or *Kleindeutschland* embracing the German Confederation outside the Habsburg Empire. Then there was the fear that political revolution would precipitate social revolution, fear inspired by socialists like Marx. This nervousness encouraged the idea that the ruling princely families could not be

Dealing with Examination Questions

replaced. The alarms and disagreements delayed the reaching of decisions by the politically inexperienced parliamentarians. By the time a new constitution had been framed the old ruling families had regained their confidence through their ability to retain the loyalty of the states' armies. By a tiny majority the throne of Germany was offered to the King of Prussia. The offer was rejected by this essentially autocratic monarch. There was no one else to turn to.

3 What effects did the events of 1848–50 in Germany have on the movements towards German unity?

The 1848 Revolution in Germany initially offered the prospect of a united German nation embracing all German speakers within the framework of a written liberal constitution. The first of these prospects was destroyed by the revival of the Habsburg Empire under Franz Joseph, the second by the refusal of the King of Prussia to accept the Frankfurt constitution. However, by 1850 it was clear that if a German nation was to be established it would be under Prussian leadership. At the same time the concept of universal suffrage had been established by the Frankfurt Parliament and even, in a weighted form, by the Prussian constitution. The importance of armies in determining the future had also been clearly indicated between 1848 and 1850. In addition, the attempted Erfurt Union of 1850 had demonstrated the ambition of the Hohenzollerns to dominate *Kleindeutschland*. Although the 1848 revolution failed in its objectives, the outcome indicated the importance of Prussia's future role in the movement towards Germany's unity.

4 How far did Bismarck's success between 1862 and 1870 depend on the errors and misjudgements of others?

Between these dates Bismarck enjoyed considerable success in both his internal and foreign policies. Having been appointed Chancellor as the result of an internal crisis, he initially ignored the opposition of the National Liberals in parliament and then won their support thanks to his successful foreign policy. It was the action of Christian IX of Denmark which precipitated the Austro-Prussian takeover of Schleswig-Holstein. Certainly it was Austrian and French misunderstanding of Bismarck's intentions combined with Austrian mishandling of Schleswig-Holstein which enabled Bismarck to provoke war over this issue. Military victory produced a Prussian absorption of North Germany. Napoleon III's refusal to be content with a diplomatic victory over the issue of a German king on the throne of Spain led to the Franco-Prussian War and the creation of the Prussian-dominated German *Reich*. However, ultimately for all Bismarck's success in exploiting his enemy's mistakes he was dependent on the power of the Prussian army to bring him success.

Confederation to Empire

5 Was the *Kulturkampf* Bismarck's most serious mistake in domestic policy?

Arguably Bismarck introduced the *Kulturkampf* because he identified the Catholic Centre Party as a threat – owing its first allegiance to the international church rather than the nation state. As a policy it was certainly mistaken. Persecution of the Catholic Church contributed to the growth and unity of the Centre Party and by 1877–8 Bismarck recognised his failure. The anti-Catholic laws were allowed to lapse, but by setting German against German Bismarck sacrificed some of the sense of unity which had been won in the war against the French. Additionally, German Catholics learnt to distrust the state. However, this was not Bismarck's only mistake. The introduction of protectionism in 1879, while profiting the grain producers in particular, was expensive for the majority of German consumers.

In 1878 Bismarck also introduced his anti-socialist legislation. This was certainly as mistaken as the *Kulturkampf*. The *SPD* grew rapidly but in reality never represented a genuine threat to the *Reich*. Nevertheless Bismarck's policies set the tone for successive German governments' attitudes to the Socialists.

6 How accurate is it to describe the years 1871–90 as the Age of Bismarck?

The success of Prussia in the wars of 1866 and 1870 had demonstrated that Germany was the most potent military power in Europe. Until his fall from power in 1890 it was Bismarck, the German Chancellor, who effectively controlled this force. Bismarck identified Germany as a territorially satisfied power and was determined to retain the German position by the preservation of peace in Europe. He was the moving spirit behind the *Dreikaiserbund*. He was chairman at the 1878 Congress of Berlin which produced peace in the Balkans lasting nearly forty years. He instigated the Dual Alliance with the Austrian Empire, initially to restrain Austrian Balkan ambitions. In the short period when he backed colonial expansion, 1884–5, Germany acquired far more colonial territory, in Africa, than during the twenty years of *Weltpolitik* 1894–1914. He was determined to prevent the convergence of two potential conflicts, the Franco-German and the Austro-Russian. His success meant that for these 19 years, apart from the short lived Russo-Turkish war, Europe enjoyed peace.

7 To what extent were the problems facing the rulers of Germany in the period 1890–1914 the legacy of Bismarck?

The legacy of Bismarck contributed to the problems of Germany after 1890, but the actions of Germany's rulers made the problems greater.

Dealing with Examination Questions

Bismarck had developed the constitution of the *Reich*; arguably it required a man with Bismarck's ability as Chancellor to make it function. After 1890 the inconsistency of William II increased the problem. Bismarck introduced protectionism which largely benefited the East Prussian Junkers at the expense of the majority of consumers. The situation was improved by Caprivi's trade treaties but exacerbated by the new tariff laws of 1902. Bismarck had allied the *Reich* with Austria–Hungary with the intention of restraining Austria in the Balkans. Under his successors the restraint weakened and Germany itself became increasingly involved in Balkan problems. Under William II the industrialisation of Germany was rapid, producing an ever larger industrial working class and socialist movement. One of the aims of the fleet building programme was to provide the workers with security of employment. However, this in turn produced new problems. Relations with Britain deteriorated. At the same time the *Reich* government faced increasing difficulty in funding its programmes.

8 How justified is the claim that 'The domestic policies of German governments in the period 1878–1914 were motivated by exaggerated fears of socialism'?

Bismarck introduced anti-socialist legislation in 1878 because he identified the *SPD* as part of an international revolutionary movement which thus posed a threat to the *Reich*. In the 1880s he introduced a social welfare programme to win the working classes away from the *SPD*. After his fall from power in 1890 the anti-socialist laws were allowed to lapse, but the success of the *SPD* in 1893 reawakened the fears of William II and successive governments. Thus one motive for building the German navy was to provide security of employment and in this way wean the workers from socialism. There was reluctance to expand the army since it was feared that its reliability would be lessened by the recruitment of the politically-conscious working-class troops. However, there were other motives behind domestic politics. The 1902 tariff laws, for example, were introduced largely to please the right-wing Junkers even though this produced higher food prices. In any case, in 1914 it was clearly demonstrated that the fear of socialism had been exaggerated when the *SPD*, the largest party in the *Reichstag*, showed its loyalty to the German Empire by voting for war credits.

Specimen Essay Answer

What were the motives behind German foreign policy between 1871 and 1914?

In 1871 Bismarck had achieved the creation of a Prussian dominated German Empire. In his eyes Germany was now a satisfied power with no

Confederation to Empire

ambition for further territorial expansion. The motivation behind his foreign policy for the remainder of his period of power was therefore to preserve this Empire.

In at least two respects Germany was potentially vulnerable. Firstly it was a state in central Europe without natural frontiers and surrounded by major powers. Secondly Bismarck had deprived France of much of Alsace and Lorraine and there was every prospect that France, in the future, would mount a war to recover the lost provinces. To meet this eventuality Bismarck was determined to keep France isolated since without an ally she posed no real threat to Germany. By achieving the *Dreikaiserbund* in 1873 with Russia and Austria–Hungary, Bismarck was able to counter both potential dangers.

Unfortunately for the Chancellor, the Three Emperors' League broke down in 1878 as a result of Austro-Russian rivalry in the Balkans, and at the same time Russo-German relations deteriorated. In 1879, Bismarck entered Germany into the Dual Alliance with Austria–Hungary. One of his major reasons for concluding the Alliance was to be able to restrain Austria in the Balkans and in the long run to restore the *Dreikaiserbund*. This was achieved in 1881 and Bismarck further cemented relations with Russia by persuading German financiers to back a loan to Russia.

In the mid-1880s Bismarck supported German colonial expansion in Africa, culminating in the 1884–5 Berlin Conference. The reasons for this were that Bismarck was responding to domestic pressure to establish new markets for German industry while at the same time improving relations with France by supporting French ambitions in Africa. This policy did not survive the election of the anti-German Freycinet government in France.

Bismarck suffered another setback when the *Dreikaiserbund* again broke down in 1887. He wanted to preserve the Dual Alliance with Austria but not sacrifice good relations with Russia. So within six months he promoted the so-called Reinsurance Treaty with Alexander III. This secured Germany against a Franco-Russian alliance but also committed the *Reich* to supporting Russian ambitions in Bulgaria against the perceived interests of Austria. However, in spite of the apparently contrary nature of this arrangement Bismarck had succeeded in his major objectives when he fell from power in 1890.

From 1890 the motives inspiring German foreign policy certainly changed. Following the lead of William II, German statesmen were now anxious to secure for Germany a world role commensurate with its industrial and military position. The Kaiser proclaimed 'Germany has become *Weltreich*', but there was no clearly identified means of achieving this objective.

It was now felt that there was no chance of Tsarist Russia coming to terms with Republican France so, in 1890, the Reinsurance Treaty was not renewed. But by 1894 a Franco-Russian alliance had been concluded and Germany's position in central Europe inevitably weakened. Afterwards William II tried to rebuild Russo-German friendship through a personal relationship with Nicholas II, but pro-Russian policies were never pursued consistently.

Germany's determination to exercise a world role was almost bound to produce clashes with Britain and the first occurred over the 'Kruger Telegram', in which William II expressed support for the President of the Transvaal in 1896. Anglo-German relations worsened as a result of the growth of the German navy and, although periodic attempts were made to reach a compromise, again the policy was pursued inconsistently.

Germany's ambition to increase its influence in Africa led to the Moroccan crises of 1905 and 1911, worsening relations with France. In the same period increasing Anglo-German tension was a factor in persuading Britain to sign treaties of friendship with France in 1904 and Russia in 1907. In turn the Anglo-French relationship was strengthened by the Moroccan crises. This situation produced a sense of 'encirclement' in Germany and tied the country more closely to the one remaining secure ally – Austria–Hungary.

Thus in 1914 Germany was prepared to accept the risk of a European war by backing Austria against Serbia. However, this was not the only reason for Germany's actions in the summer of 1914. Many in the German establishment now felt that a successful war was the only way to solve the *Reich*'s domestic political and social problems.

Bismarck had clear goals, pursued them consistently and on the whole successfully. After 1890 the goals were no longer clearly identified. Consequently no consistent policy was pursued and the outcome was a war which destroyed the German state.

BIBLIOGRAPHY

Understandably there is a vast wealth of literature about this period of German history. The following list is intended as a guide to some of the more accessible and readable studies.

V.R. Berghahn: *Germany and the Approach of War in 1914* (St Martin's Press 1973). A German historian examines the factors which led to the outbreak of war in 1914.

W.A. Carr: *A History of Germany 1815–1990* (Edward Arnold 1991). An outline history of Germany in the nineteenth and twentieth centuries first published in 1969 and subsequently updated and reprinted.

Gordon A. Craig: *Germany 1866–1945* (Oxford University Press 1978). A book that every student of the period should read. It provides a clear and stimulating account of the evolution of Germany from Bismarck to Hitler.

Fritz Fischer: *Germany's Aims in the First World War* (Chatto & Windus 1967). He puts forward the thesis that the policies of the German Empire were clearly to blame for the outbreak of war in 1914.

Immanuel Geiss: *German Foreign Policy 1871–1914* (Routledge & Kegan Paul 1976). A concise but valuable account of the factors determining German foreign policy in this period.

Michael Gorman: *The Unification of Germany* (Cambridge University Press 1989). A concise treatment with documents and commentary.

T.S. Hamerow: *Restoration, Revolution, Reaction* (Princeton University Press 1966). An examination of the social, economic and political circumstances producing change in Germany between 1815 and German unification.

Paul Kennedy: *The Rise of Anglo-German Antagonism 1860–1914* (Allen & Unwin 1982). A detailed examination of the course of Anglo-German relations and how they contributed to the outbreak of war in 1914.

Giles MacDonogh: *Prussia, The Perversion of an Idea* (Sinclair Stevenson 1994, also in Mandarin paperbacks). This study poses a number of questions about developments in Prussia and the role of Prussia in Germany.

Bibliography

Alan Palmer: *Bismarck* (Weidenfeld & Nicolson 1976). A lucid study of Bismarck's life and his achievements in the national and international fields.

Alan Palmer: *The Kaiser* (Weidenfeld & Nicolson 1978). A very readable biography of the life of William II and an account of the impact he had on the nature of German politics during his reign.

Eda Sagarra: *An Introduction to Nineteenth Century Germany* (Longman 1980). A very useful survey of nineteenth-century German history which includes economic and social as well as political developments.

A.J.P. Taylor: *Bismarck, the Man and the Statesman* (Hamish Hamilton 1955). The first modern biography of Bismarck by a British historian, occasionally controversial but very readable.

Brian Warner: *Bismarck* (Blackwell Historical Association 1985). A sound summary of Bismarck's career and the varying historical interpretations. He does not support H.-U. Wehler's view of Bismarck's imperial policies.

Hans-Ulrich Wehler: *The German Empire 1871–1918* (Berg 1985). A controversial study which argues that when Germany entered the twentieth century the ruling élite succeeded in withstanding the pressure for democratisation by using Bonapartist methods.

D.G. Williamson: *Bismarck and Germany 1862–1890* (Longman 1986). A brief and clear treatment of Bismarck's role in Germany in this period – contains a helpful set of documents and a very good bibliography.

Students will also benefit from consulting the two relevant texts in the Access to History Series:

Geoff Layton: *From Bismarck to Hitler, Germany 1870–1933* (Hodder & Stoughton 1995).

Andrina Stiles: *The Unification of Germany 1815–1890* (Hodder & Stoughton 1990).

INDEX

Alexander II of Russia 62, 69, 71
Alexander III of Russia 62, 72, 76
Algeçiras Conference 100, 103, 104, 108
Alsace and Lorraine 5
Alvensleben Convention 36, 39
America 56, 103
Anglo-Boer War 99
Anglo-Portuguese Treaty 73
Anti-Semitism 49, 52
Augustenburg, Duke of 36
Austrian Empire 3, 5, 6, 10, 17, 18, 23, 25, 26, 30, 32, 33, 36, 37, 38, 39, 40, 41, 42, 56, 61, 62, 69, 71, 72, 75, 89, 94, 108, 111

Baden 3, 38
Bavaria 4, 10, 38, 43, 46
Beaconsfield, Lord 69, 70
Belgium 74, 105
Benedetti 37, 44, 46
Berlin Civic Guard 15
Berlin Congress 62, 69
Bethmann-Hollweg 6, 78, 85, 108, 111
Bismarck 5, 28, 30–34, 36–48, 49–59, 88, 114, 115
Björkö Treaty 87, 93
Bosnia 101, 108
Britain (England) 6, 11, 43, 66, 70, 71, 73, 76, 79, 85, 87, 88, 89, 90, 95, 96, 97, 98, 100, 101, 102, 103, 107, 109, 110, 118
Brunswick 4
Bulgaria 69, 74, 75
Bülow, Bernhard von 6, 24, 77, 79, 83, 84, 100, 103, 104

Camphausen 10
Caprivi 6, 77, 78, 79, 87
Centre Party 49
Chamberlain, Joseph 97, 98
Christian IX of Denmark 36
Churchill, Winston 118

Daily Telegraph 78, 83, 84
Denmark 11, 36
Dreikaiserbund 6, 61, 62, 63, 70
Dual Alliance 6, 62, 70

Ems Telegram 45
Entente Cordiale 100, 102
Erfurt Union 4, 23

Fisher, Sir John 118
France 4, 5, 10, 30, 36, 42, 48, 56, 61, 63, 65, 66, 69, 71, 72, 74, 75, 76, 92, 100, 101, 102, 103, 104, 105, 108, 109, 117
Franco-Russian Alliance 100
Frankfurt Parliament 4, 10–12, 18, 19, 21
Frankfurt, Peace of 37
Franz Ferdinand, Archduke of Austria 7, 101, 108
Franz Joseph II, Habsburg Emperor 11
Frederick III of Germany 50, 74
Frederick William IV of Prussia 10, 12, 18, 20, 23, 28, 30

Gägern, Heinrich von 17
Gastein, Convention of 36, 40
German Confederation (Bund) 3, 10–11

134

Index

Gladstone, William   71
Goltz, Count   42, 43
Gortschakov, Prince   39, 42, 61
Grey, Sir Edward   103, 109

Haldane, Lord   101
Hanover   23–24
Hansemann   10
Heligoland Treaty   87, 89
Hesse   3
Hesse-Casel   4
Hesse-Darmstadt   43
Hohenlohe, Chlodwig   6, 77
Holland   74, 105
Holy Roman Empire   3

Italy   61, 62, 69, 72, 89, 94

Jameson Raid   87, 95

Karl Anton, Prince   45
Karlsruhe   3
Kiaochow   87, 95, 96
Kiel   40, 41
Kiel Canal   41, 89
Königgrätz   37
Kruger Telegram   87, 94, 95
Kulturkampf   5, 49, 53, 54, 61

Leopold of Hohenzollern-Sigmaringen   37
Lloyd George, David   101, 109
London, Treaty of   40
Luxemburg   43, 105

Malmö   11
Manteuffel   23, 32
Marx, Karl   20
Metternich   3, 4
Morocco   7, 100, 102, 103, 108, 109

Napoleon III of France   41, 42, 43
National Liberal Party   49
Navy Laws   77, 107

Nicholas I of Russia   23
Nicholas II of Russia   87, 92, 111, 112
North German Confederation   37, 49, 51

Olmütz   23, 24, 30

Poland   39
Portugal   73, 74
Prague, Peace of   37
Prussia   3–5, 10–12, 13, 15, 23, 24, 28, 31, 32, 38, 104
Prussian United Diet   30

Radowitz, Joseph von   23
Reinsurance Treaty   6, 62, 75, 87, 89
Reichstag   6, 24, 49, 56, 77, 78, 79, 81, 86
Revolutions of 1848   4
Russia   4, 6, 7, 11, 36, 39, 42, 61, 62, 69, 70, 71, 72, 75, 76, 87, 88, 92, 100, 101, 111, 120

Salisbury, Lord   89, 90, 92, 95, 96, 99
Sanders, Liman von   101, 110
Saxony   23–24
Schleswig-Holstein   11, 31, 36, 40
Schlieffen, Alfred von   7, 100, 101, 105
Schwarzenburg, Felix   23
Serbia   101, 111, 112
Silesia   13
Social Democratic Party   5, 50, 77, 78, 79, 81, 85
Spain   74, 108
Switzerland   94

Tangier   100
Tirpitz, Alfred von   77, 82, 87, 96, 97
Triple Alliance   62, 72
Triple Entente   101, 102
Turkey   67, 69, 75

Venetia   41

Confederation to Empire

Verona, Treaty of 36
Vienna, Congress of 3

Weltpolitik 6, 104
Westphalia 13
William I, King of Prussia, Kaiser of Germany 6, 30, 36, 37, 42, 50, 69

William II, Kaiser of Germany 6, 50, 58, 84, 77–86, 87–99, 100–113
Windthorst, Ludwig 49, 65
Württemberg 3, 12, 38

Zanzibar 87, 90
Zollverein 4, 23, 25, 30, 34, 41